4

FOR THE
MOUNTAINTOP
RETREATS

My Journey, Our Journey, Your Journey

TRANSFORMED BY CHRIST FROM
FRIENDS TO SISTERS

Ellen Mongan

ISBN 978-1-68526-725-4 (Paperback)
ISBN 978-1-68526-726-1 (Digital)

Covenant Books
11661 Hwy 707
Murrells Inlet, SC 29576
www.covenantbooks.com

In this book, Ellen shares with her enthusiasm and candor the joy of finding God and going where he leads you. As a woman who has my own group of retreat friends, I can assure you that the wisdom Ellen shares is an important part in the journey of falling more in love with Jesus while building deep sisterhood along the way.

—Rachel Balducci, author of Make My Life Simple, and No Such Thing as Ordinary (Ave Maria Press, Spring 2022)

I personally know Anne, Debbie and Ellen, and Pat. They are all beautiful women whose physical and spiritual beauty are resident in their deep love for Jesus and their docility to the Holy Spirit. This love and docility has led them all to some extraordinary grace and blessing that can only be found in God's Kingdom. Their 50+ retreats together over more than 20 years have for them been a wonderful journey together. Ellen, in her own poetic style, has captured the heart of their love and their journey. Please read this book slowly and when you have some time to join them in their journey and smell the flowers.

"I have heard of Thee by the hearing of the ear, but now my eye sees Thee." Job 42:5

Bob Garrett
Alleluia Community July 23, 2019

Ellen's book very much reminds me of the movie, "Steel Magnolias". But there is a big difference. This true story includes a most important spiritual element—helping one another grow in holiness and reach union with God. This book shows what the gift of holy friendships can accomplish in our lives and the critical importance of making informal but intentional relationships a priority as we journey together toward heaven.

Dan Almeter
Elder in Alleluia Community

Ellen Mongan's **4 for the Mountaintop Retreats** is an exciting spiritual journey encouraging anyone who wants to grow in holiness with real spiritual sisters helping each other attain this goal. The openness of Ellen's heart and her 3 friends inspires the reader to become more intimate with JESUS through scripture, the saints and poetry. The lived-out examples from these 4 women encourages us to lift up our minds and hearts to make a journey up the mountain with JESUS, drawing closer and closer to HIM along the way. I encourage anyone who is serious about spiritual life to be inspired by the journey of these four women and then make it happen in your own life. Ellen gives a true guide for this experience.

Father Ted Hochstatter

Ellen Mongan is a prime example of apple pie and motherhood in fifth gear- ever energized and ready. She is also a terrific wife, a woman of expectant faith and a great sister in the Lord. She is on duty 24/7 to share in word and print her blessed life and Gods' unmerited favor with any who will "come and see" and *taste the goodness of the Lord.*

Through Ellen's' life experience and sharing in her new book, women will come to a better awareness of Gods' plan and provision for Christian womanhood. Of course, faith and enthusiasm are not gender limited but rather quite contagious to all. Ellen has plenty of to pour out on anyone looking for the "more".

In the days coming each of us will need to dig deep and lean and trust more in the Lord and His blessings.

Gary Garner author of
Swept Up by the Spirit Journey of Transformation
and
Journey to Glory—Contending for the Faith.

This book is dedicated to Anne Shea, Debbie Cosper, and Pat Maranda—my three "four for the Mt. Top sisters." We began the journey as young mothers with a house full of babies. We have traveled together through all seasons of life. We have been a listening ear, a helping hand, and a word of advice to each other. Our relationships have passed the test of time. I know that I can always count on you. We hope that our journey will never end. You are more than friends and sisters in Christ. To me, Anne, Debbie, and Pat, we are family. Now we pass the wisdom we have learned down to the next generation. Thank you for accompanying me on the adventure of a lifetime up the mountain into the heart of God.

This book is also dedicated to our beloved husbands, four dear men who sacrificed many long weekends in allowing us to have our four "for the mountaintop" retreats. It was truly a gift of laying down their lives, selflessly putting aside their own plans for those weekends, out of love for us. It was so appreciated; that special time we had together as women was treasured. We could not have gone away if it weren't for our men. Knowing they were making sure things were taken care of at home gave us the peace to leave our homes and families behind and enter into God's presence without a worry or care. I always came back with a new appreciation for my husband and family. There truly is no place like home.

Also, I want to thank my husband, Deacon Pat Mongan, for hours of editing, reediting, proofreading, and formatting this book!

Lastly, I want to thank my son, Tyler Patrick William Mongan, for his wisdom in guiding me to divide this book into three sections.

My Journey
Our Journey
Your Journey!

It gave me the ability to add a Bible study as a guide, which became the meat of the book.

After six days, Jesus took Peter, James, and John his brother and led them up a high mountain by themselves. And he was transfigured before them; his face shone like the sun and his clothes became white as light. And behold, Moses and Elijah appeared to them, conversing with him. Then Peter said to Jesus in reply, "Lord, it is good that we are here. If you wish, I will make three tents here, one for you, one for Moses, and one for Elijah." While he was still speaking, behold, a bright cloud cast a shadow over them, then from the cloud came a voice that said, "This is my beloved Son, with whom I am well pleased; listen to him." When the disciples heard this, they fell prostrate and were very much afraid. But Jesus came and touched them, saying, "Rise, and do not be afraid." And when the disciples raised their eyes, they saw no one else but Jesus alone. As they were coming down from the mountain, Jesus charged them, "Do not tell the vision to anyone until the Son of Man has been raised from the dead."
—Matthew 17:1–9

We all need to go apart, to ascend the mountain in a space of silence, to find ourselves and better perceive the voice of the Lord. This we do in prayer. But we cannot stay there! Encounter with God in prayer inspires us anew to "descend the mountain" and return to the plain where we meet many brothers weighed down by fatigue, sickness, injustice, ignorance, poverty both material and spiritual.
—Pope Francis, "Angelus" (March 16, 2014)

CONTENTS

Part 3: Your Journey: The Eight Climbs

INTRODUCTION

Have you been to the mountaintop with God? Think of how exciting it must have been to be selected by Jesus, the Son of God, to be one of His twelve disciples and then to have walked with Him, talked with Him, and to be invited to go up to the mountain with Him. I wonder if Peter, James, and John were able to sleep a wink the night before the journey. I know that I would not have.

What a story they would have to tell the other nine disciples who were not on the guest list. Their lives were never the same again as they touched a piece of heaven that day. They even overheard a conference call made by Jesus to Moses and Elijah and viewed it with their own eyes. No wonder they were not too anxious to return to life as they knew it back down the mountain. They wanted to stay forever—wouldn't you?

There are times in our life where we, too, are asked by Jesus to go to the mountaintop and meet Him face to face—times like retreats, conferences, prayer meetings, missions, or just Bible studies. Mountaintop experiences give us the chance to quiet our souls and hear Jesus speak to us a little clearer than in the busyness of everyday life. If we accept the invitation to go to the mountaintop with our God, our lives are changed forever. I highly recommend it.

One of my favorite mountaintop experiences is to get alone with God with my three best friends, a group which we call "4 for the Mountaintop." We try to go twice a year. These sisters and I have been journeying to the mountains for over thirty years. We have laughed together, cried together, been pregnant together, raised babies together, shared our wisdom, shared our hearts, and, most importantly, shared our walk with Jesus together. I trust these ladies with my life. We have all grown closer to Jesus because of it.

This book, *4 for the Mountaintop*, is threefold. It begins with my journey toward God. Then this journey converged with three other women who also were on a journey with God. We all continued on our own journey, but this enhanced it. We began with friendship, which grew into sisterhood, and then we began to go away on retreats. God knit out hearts together, and we all grew closer to Him. This adventure for us blossomed when we answered God's call to go away with Him to the mountaintop.

Now is the time that God calls me to tell both the story of my journey to the heart of God and the birth of 4 for the Mountaintop. It has been the adventure of a lifetime. I am glad I accepted Jesus's invitation.

Lastly, I have written eight *climbs*, written in a Bible-study format. They are meant to guide you on your own journey and provide encouragement as you strive to reach the top of your mountain.

Jesus invites all to get away with Him and go to the mountaintop. Like Peter, James, and John, will you accept the invitation? I highly recommend inviting your three best friends to take the journey with you. Your *yes* will also begin the adventure of a lifetime. What story will you have to tell? I cannot wait to read all about it.

Let's pray: Dear Jesus, let us never be too busy to hear you say, "*Let us go to the mountaintop together.*" Let us pack light with a heart ready to be filled with your love and ears opened to obedience. May we never return home the same.

When was the last time you got away with God to seek His face? Is He calling your name? Linger no longer—you're invited! I encourage you to say *yes*. Jesus is waiting there for you. Can you hear Him say, "Come away with me, my love!"

PART 1

My Journey

CHAPTER 1

In God Alone I Place My Trust

Ellen's Testimony

Every Christian faith walk takes you on a journey, journeys where you are asked to take Jesus's nail-scarred hand and trust Him to lead you. Jesus leads you to the very heart of our loving Heavenly Father.

I was born and baptized into the Catholic faith. As a cradle Catholic, my faith was nourished through a praying grandma's good example and the instruction of the nuns in Catholic school. I can still remember the nuns saying, "Who made you? God made you. Why did God make you? God made you to know Him, to love Him, to serve Him, and to be happy with Him one day in heaven." I grew to know and love my Catholic faith. I longed to receive Jesus in the Eucharist. What a glorious day it was when I, dressed all in white as a bride, walked to the altar, singing, "Jesus, Jesus, come to me." God knew it was truly my heart's desire, and He answered that prayer.

As I received Jesus's "body, blood, soul, and divinity" for the first time, the truth of our faith was written on my soul. Jesus revealed Himself to me. I gave my life to Him, and He began to lead me. I went to daily mass, frequented the sacrament of reconciliation, sang to Jesus, and prayed about everything.

High school found me in a public school where it was not in vogue to be a committed Catholic. In order to be popular, I went undercover, but my faith suffered greatly. My family went to Mass on Sunday, and I continued to pray before I went to bed. However, I had no support from other Catholics, no opportunity for daily

Eucharist, and I did not grow in the faith. The day I graduated from high school, my family moved back to the South. I tried a college in Georgia and one in Florida, and both were a culture shock; drugs, drinking, and sex were rampant, and I was appalled. I knew it would be impossible for me to grow close to Jesus in this environment. I left college behind to take a different path.

I moved to Florida to fulfill my dream to be a stewardess with a friend. We were soon flying the friendly skies as flight attendants for Air Florida. Again, my faith suffered, and Jesus was no longer first in my life. The unfortunate part was, I was not even aware of it!

At age nineteen, I met and fell in love with the man of my dreams, Patrick, who was studying to be a physician at University of Miami. He happened to be Peggy's cousin. During this season of my life, God tried to get my attention through a dream. In the dream I was stirring some cookie dough in a bowl. As I gazed into the bowl, Jesus appeared, saying, "*I am the way, and the truth, and the life. The only way to the Father is through me.*" Since this was not an ordinary experience for me, I sought advice. However, I did not get clear direction, so I dismissed it. Pat and I married on May 1, 1974. After a one-month honeymoon and graduation, we moved to Gainesville, Florida, for Pat's residency.

We soon had a little boy and a little girl and lived in suburbia. In a worldly sense, we had made it. I was so happy that I went back to church. In a four-year lapse of practicing my faith, the charismatic renewal had evolved. I went to a prayer meeting where a gal read the same scripture from my dream. I knew I was home. It was on that day that I gave my heart back to Jesus. I promised Him that I did not care who knew I was a Catholic and that I would live for Him.

When Pat decided to go into practice, I prayed we would go to where Pat—then a pagan—would find Jesus. After a year in Vernal, Utah, Pat gave his heart to Jesus too. Together we made the decision to move back to the South to be close to family and to join Alleluia, a charismatic community in Augusta, Georgia. God blessed us with many children, friendships, teachings, and great graces. God trained us up, nourished us, and established us. In Alleluia, people were trying to live radically for Jesus. Then God called Pat to become a deacon. We both embraced full-time ministry and agreed to pour our lives into building the church. In the Catholic Church, God had a purpose for my life.

I believe God has called me to pass the faith down to the next generation and to help young mothers find the joy in their vocation as wife and mother. I have been blessed with the opportunity to speak about Jesus on TV, radio, moms' clubs, churches, and through the books and Bible studies I have written.

You never know where God will take you. I have journeyed to mountaintops of great joy, into valleys of tears and sadness, and through deserts of loneliness, waiting until God parts the Red Sea. I have learned that in the crucible of suffering, you get to know God for yourself. He alone will teach you how to walk on the water, if you keep your eyes on Him. When you begin to sink, He will send a lifeboat in the form of other committed followers.

No one can walk the journey alone. I wake up every morning to pray and seek the face of Jesus and to take a strong hold of his nail-scarred hand. I ask Him, "How can I serve you today?" I try to attend Mass daily and confession frequently; that is where the grace is. I know I need Him. In Him alone I place my trust. I want Him to be my everything!

*****

I Offer You My Nothingness

*Jesus, I offer You myself today, in my **nothingness**.*
As I begin a new day, let me live in You, for You, and through You.
I come as a beggar asking You, Jesus, to use me as a vessel of Your love.
I seek You alone…please fill me with Your unending love,
so I can pour it out on everyone I meet.
*If You do not fill me, I will have **nothing** to give them.*
Let me be the hands of Veronica today to wipe the face of a stranger who
    is suffering,
because that it was You did, Jesus!

Let me be Simeon to help shoulder someone's Cross on my journey today,
because that is what You did, Jesus!

Let me be hospitable like Martha, Mary, and Lazarus to friends
and to strangers alike today.
Because that is what You did, Jesus!

Let me give as the "widow's mite" and not count the cost.
Today may I give not only of my treasure but also,
let me take the time to use my gifts to bless others today,
because that is what You did, Jesus!

Let me always see another's need as greater than my own today and every
*   day,*
because that is what You did, Jesus!

Let me be Your disciple.
Let me be willing to tirelessly teach the faith in love to those who seek
*   Your truth.*
Because that is what You did, Jesus!

Let me be Your words of wisdom to the next generation.
Let me reach out to them with motherly arms,
because that is what Your Mother did, Jesus!

Let me be bold yet gentle like Your servant Esther,
if I come face-to-face with a Royal King or a little child. Let me be kind
*   and submissive,*
yet prudent like Your servant Abigail to the strangers along life's journey.
Let me be a woman of faith like Sarah, of patience like Elizabeth, and
*   honoring like Ruth.*
Most of all, Jesus, let me always completely surrender to Your plan for my
*   life,*
just as the Blessed Mother did.

Give me eyes to see all I encounter through Your eyes,
because Your eyes are eyes of love and compassion.
Let me not miss the present moment to see You in each person I meet.
Since that moment may never come my way again, let me show them
*   Your loving care,*
because that is what You would do, Jesus!

*Give me ears to hear Your voice as I speak to each stranger or friend I
    meet today.*
*Give me the ability to take the time to listen between the lines as they
    speak.*
Give me an understanding heart by listening intently,
since that conversation may never take place again.
Give me the self-control and patience to take the time now,
because that is what You would do, Jesus!

Let me be Your hands today, Jesus,
hands that willingly meet the needs of those You bring to me.
Give me hardworking hands and a giving heart to serve them.
I know this opportunity to serve them may not come my way ever again.
So give me the grace to say yes without any stress.
*One thing I know: if You want me to serve them, You will give me the
    grace I need.*
*You will also keep me in perfect peace, so help me to have a Servant's
    heart,*
because You would do that, Jesus!

Let me open my heart wide today to love and be loved, out of love for You.
Freely pour into my heart Your love and fill me to overflowing.
*Let me not keep this love for myself. Rather, let me pour this love out on
    all I meet,*
for I know I may not pass this way again,
Because You would do that, Jesus!

*I am nothing without You, and without You today, I can do nothing good
    at all.*
I begin this day empty of myself before You,
and to give You my willing yes! I surrender to Your will.
*I call upon You again to fill me with Your love, because You are the source
    of love.*
Let me love Your people today and be Your vessel of love.
Let me draw others to Your love.

Let me love others into the Kingdom.
"Here I am, Lord, I have come to do Your will today."
*My willingness and my **nothingness** are all I have to give You.*

Jesus, I love You. Amen.

CHAPTER 2

In the Beginning

As I sit down, putting pen to paper to tell what God has done with us on the "4 for the Mountaintop" retreats, I am in awe of our Lord Jesus Christ, our Retreat Master! These retreats were a journey for us led by God. Thankfully, He still leads us on. There is no denying this was a work of God. Proverbs 19:9 tells us, "*The human heart plans the way, but the LORD directs the steps.*" Our Heavenly Father has directed our path to the mountaintop and to the heart of God. All four of us agree that our God is good, all the time, all day long!

Where does one begin to tell about a journey that spans more than thirty years? I am never at a loss for words, and I am reminded of the lyrics from my favorite movie *The Sound of Music*. The words are "*Let's start at the very beginning; it is a very good place to start.*" I am often found quoting from *The Sound of Music*, so this is perfectly normal for me. Yes, this movie made quite an impression on me. As a young girl, I aspired to be a nun—that is, until I met my beloved Patrick. So I find the words "the very beginning" a perfect introduction. Not only has *The Sound of Music* made an impression on me, it has become the life I have lived here on this Earth.

I, Ellen, am the mountaintop sister (like Maria in the movie) who had the house of children—seven, to be exact. Even though my husband did not blow a whistle, he did run a tight ship. I was the people pleaser who tried desperately to be holy. My AAA-type personality, mixed with the high standards of perfection I shared with my husband, made me the one who needed time-outs the most. I needed time to rest, refresh, restore, and retreat in Jesus. It was an added bonus that I could take those time-outs with my three best friends, Anne, Debbie, and Pat.

We always rejoice when we leave for mountaintop retreat. This is a time we all look forward to, to prepare for and delight in. Over the course of these thirty-plus years, we have made over fifty retreats together. And now, after all the years of this blessed journey of grace, God has called me to share the Good News. Through the pages of this book, I hope to convey the message that sisters in Christ need sisters in Christ. I will attempt to explain the how, the when, and the why of our "4 for the Mountaintop" retreats. I hope to answer the questions: *Why are retreats important for Christian sisters? How do I initiate them? Who can help me?*

I always say that your journey takes you to your ministry. My ministry is to women. God has called me to encourage and to teach as a "Titus 2" mentor:

> *Similarly, older women should be reverent in their behavior, not slanderers, not addicted to drink, teaching what is good, so that they may train younger women to love their husbands and children, to be self-controlled, chaste, good homemakers, under the control of their husbands, so that the word of God may not be discredited.* (Titus 2:3–5)

He has called me to encourage and teach moms and wives to be the best mom and wife they can be. God has indeed called me to teach women to be the best woman they can be. Becoming the best we can be is a process. There are no shortcuts in the spiritual walk. It is a daily decision to seek God's face, read His word, live his Word, and receive the sacraments. It is a decision to do what the Blessed Mother said at the wedding feast of Cana, "Do whatever He tells you." The road is sometimes long, and the road is sometimes hard. The walk with Christ involves daily laying down our life, a daily decision to love God, and a daily decision to love one another.

One day, my Heavenly Father said to me, "*You cannot be holy, until you are whole.*" As I questioned in my heart, "How, Lord?" He seemed to say, "*I love you into wholeness.*" In fact, I believe that God changes us from within as we spend time with Him. Did you know that we cannot change our own hearts? No, only God can do that. These "4 for the Mountaintop" retreats are just the fertile ground that God uses to plant and establish us and to aid us in our journey toward wholeness in Christ. Then we begin to understand the scripture "*Christ in us is our hope of glory*" (Col. 1:27).

With God as our Retreat Master and the hand of Christ reaching out through our mountaintop sisters, our retreats have become a place where the fruit is abundant.

Yes, what a perfect recipe: God's love plus Christian sisterhood equal food for the soul. We read this in God's Word says:

> *The LORD is my shepherd; there is nothing I lack. In green pastures he makes me lie down; to still waters he leads me; he restores my soul. He guides me along right paths for the sake of his name. Even though I walk through the valley of the shadow of death, I will fear no evil, for you are with me; your rod and your staff comfort me. You set a table before me in front of my enemies; You anoint my head with oil; my cup overflows. Indeed, goodness and mercy will pursue me all the days of my life; I will dwell in the house of the LORD for endless days.* (Psalm 23)

God in His wisdom shows us in the scriptures the *why* of retreats.

Jesus took the disciples Peter, James, and John to the mountain of His transfiguration. They were the first "4 for the Mountaintop" disciples. Yes, God was showing these three best friends His agape love. He was also building their faith and binding them together in a way only God could do. We all know it was unforgettable for these three disciples. Peter, James, and John—like Anne, Debbie, Pat, and I—did not want to go home. Like Peter, they said, "*Lord, it is good that we are here*" (Matt. 17:4), and they did not want to leave. In His wisdom, Jesus said no. Instead, His disciples and His best friends would have to walk away from the mountain and go home. However, this transfiguration experience would always live in their memories to cement their faith when things got tough.

The life experiences the disciples faced—from the agony of Jesus in the garden through His betrayal, passion, and death on the cross—was a supreme test of their faith; but God's grace was sufficient. Even in the disciples' weakness, God became their strength. I can almost hear Peter say, "I knew we should have stayed with Moses and Elijah." I know that he wanted to add, "Jesus, I was right!" We too, like the three disciples of old, always have to pack our bags, say our goodbyes, and walk down the mountain back to our everyday lives. There is, however, always a new joy in our step, more life of Christ in our hearts, a deeper faith, and memories that will last forever. At the mountain retreats there have been more than enough laughter and a few tears too. This is how I am going to begin my book *4 for the Mountaintop.*

I must add one last word—I always must just ask Anne, Debbie, and Pat. I want to add that this is not a how-to formula for a Christian women's retreat. There is no formula in the Christian walk. As we all know, our Savior Jesus Christ is a personal Savior. Jesus Christ is the only way, the only truth, and the only life. This book is not for everyone or even for every sister in Christ. Our Savior knows us each by name. God the Father formed us all in our Mother's womb and knows what we need to become whole. He knows what we need to be formed in the character of Jesus Christ. God does whatever it takes to work a miracle in one's heart. He loves each of us that much!

Please glean from this book what portion God has for you. Prayerfully contemplate what you read and then ask God to speak to your heart. Finally, as the Blessed Mother Mary said, "Do whatever He tells you." He alone is God, He is our Savior, He is our Lord. To God be the glory, forever and ever. Amen.

Come Quickly, Lord Jesus!

If you came today, my Jesus,
in the stable of our hearts.
Would we be open to house you?
Or would we only give a part?
Would we follow as the shepherds?
Would we seek as the Kings?
Would we be open to listen?
Would we hear the angels sing?
Would our minds be filled with wonder?
Or would our hearts be filled with doubt?
Would we beckon you come hither?
Or would we demand that you get out?
Would we adore you as Savior?
Would we worship you as Lord?
Would we drop all to follow?
Or would we get bored?
As Christmas time approaches,
we think of the Holy Birth,
But as we examine our hearts,
Is Jesus really FIRST?

Many cried, "Lord, Lord," even in that day
and were left behind when they didn't choose your way.
The Kings had the rule.
The Pharisees had the law.
The people had the power to crucify our Lord.
But who had the victory?
Who is Lord of all?
Whose love reigns forever?
Answer, answer His call.
The time is growing shorter;
the end is drawing nearer.
They'll sound the final trumpet.
Our Jesus will be here.
Who will go to meet Him?
Who will answer His call?
Who will welcome His second coming?
Those who gave up all.

So make the stable ready.
Open the inn of your heart.
Follow the star of His Spirit
and give Him all, not part.
Will you take Jesus as your rule?
Will you take Jesus as your law?
Will you follow the Holy Spirit?
Will you make the Savior Lord?

CHAPTER 3

To Know God

St. Frances DeSales is known to have coined the phrase, "Begin in love, live in love, and end in love." Of course I am paraphrasing it. It reminds me of the first letter of John that says "*Beloved, let us love one another; for love is of God, and he who loves is born of God…for God is love*" (1 John 4:7–8). Saint Paul, a man of intellect and insight, not only describes love but defines it in a way that we can all understand:

> *Love is patient and kind; love is not jealous or boastful; it is not arrogant or rude. Love dies not insist on its own way; it is not irritable or resentful; it does not rejoice at wrong, but rejoices in the right. Love bears all things, believes all things, hopes all things, endures all things. Love never ends.* (1 Cor. 13:4–8)

Jesus himself became love in action when he willingly picked up the cross for our sins. Scripture says, "*Greater love has no man than this, that a man lay down his life for his friends*" (John 15:13). All of us, each and every person on this earth, are looking for true love. I remember a discussion I had with my husband one day over the scripture verse where Jesus gives the two greatest commandments. Dear reader, do you remember what they are? "*You shall love the Lord your God with all your heart, and with all your soul, and with all your mind… And a second is like it, you shall love your neighbor as yourself*" (Matt. 22:37–39).

My husband, Deacon Pat, commented, "Ellen, I think that is attainable." I must admit my thought was, *Only if you are Jesus or the Blessed Mother!* But I tempered my answer with this reply: "Pat, only by the grace of God." We both were able to agree that this would be a lifelong goal to try to live in love as St. Francis encouraged:

The Prayer of St. Francis

Lord, make me an instrument of your peace,
Where there is hatred, let me sow love;
Where there is injury, pardon;
Where there is doubt, faith;
Where there is despair, hope;
Where there is darkness, light;
Where there is sadness, joy;

O Divine Master,
Grant that I may not so much seek to be consoled, as to console;
To be understood as to understand;
To be loved as to love.
For it is in giving that we receive;
It is in pardoning that we are pardoned;
And it is in dying that we are born to eternal life.

Human beings need the love of God above all else. As we walk close to our Savior and as He remakes us on the inside, we become completely aware of the fact that God alone suffices. We read this in Scripture:

> *"Three times I begged the Lord about this, that it might leave me, but he said to me, 'My grace is sufficient for you, for power is made perfect in weakness.' I will rather boast most gladly of my weaknesses, in order that the power of Christ may dwell with me."* (2 Cor. 12:8–9)

I'll never forget the day that God began to draw me to a deeper walk with Him. I began to realize the truth that St. Teresa of Avila knew and expressed so well, "*Let noth-*

ing disturb you, let nothing frighten you, All things are passing away: God never changes. Patience obtains all things. Whoever has God lacks nothing; God alone suffices."

I was in the adoration chapel, one day, visiting Jesus; and the Holy Spirit spoke to me these words: "When the storms of life hit you, and they will, run to the adoration chapel." He said it because He knew that life happens. He was reminding me that at adoration is where God is to be found in the storm. That turning point in my life was the first of many times that I would run to the adoration chapel to meet my Jesus. *"He is my refuge and my strength, my help in times of trouble God is our refuge and our strength, an ever-present help in distress,"* Psalm 46:2 says. Yes, the adoration chapel has become my second home where Jesus welcomes me—sometimes with His presence, sometimes with His voice, sometimes through His word, sometimes through His people, and sometimes in the silence of my heart.

I tell people that the presence of God is great, but greater than the presence of God is in *knowing* He is there. God said to Moses from the burning bush, "I am." Moses knew it was holy ground; he was told to take off his sandals. Well, my friend, He still says, "*I am*"! Jesus said to him, "*I am the way and the truth and the life. No one comes to the Father except through me*" (John 14:6). Apart from Him, there is only nothingness.

It has become my lifelong quest to live out those two sentences from the Baltimore catechism that the nuns burned in my soul. If my over sixty brains serve me well, my Baltimore catechism went like this: "Why did God make you? God made me to know him, to love Him, and to serve Him in this world, and to be happy with Him forever in the next." I believe that those two statements sum up our entire Catholic faith in a nutshell. I say it like this: "For to know him is to love him and to love him is to serve him and one day we will be happy with him in heaven." My sister in Christ, do you know Him? Do you love Him? Do you want to serve Him? Would you like to be happy one with Jesus in heaven?

God has put on my heart this message from our old Baltimore catechism. I faithfully share it in every talk I give. I thank God for the nuns Sister Lucida, Sister Benedictus, and Sister Germaine who formed me in my Catholic faith and planted a desire to belong to God alone! In God alone I put my trust.

Do you read the Bible? Do you know that in our Catholic faith, if we go to Mass every day in the course of three years, we will have heard most of the Bible from the readings? One of my favorite Bible stories is Job. I love to tell the story of Job because it contains my favorite scripture quote of all, where Job says to God, *"I had heard of thee by the hearing of the ear, but now my eye sees thee"* (Job 42:5).

Some of you women reading this may be searching your heart right now, saying these words to yourself, "God, do I know you for myself?" I say to you, women, if you know God only through your friends or family, you may need to seek a deeper relationship with God. Our God is a personal God who wants a personal relationship with you. He knows you, He loves you, and He died for you.

Job went through the fire; he lost children, his livestock, his home, and riches. "Oh, the patience of Job," you might be saying. I say, don't feel so sorry for Job! Job, in the midst of the storm of life, ran to God. Where do you run when the storm of life hits you? Do you run to a friend, a bottle of liquor, psychiatrist, or do you run into the arms of your loving Heavenly Father? Trials are the time to cling to your God. My beloved sister, our Catholic faith teaches that trials are the time to seek God's face—in the Mass, in the confessional, in the adoration chapel, in prayer, and in God's word. *"Draw near to God and He will draw near to you,"* says James 4:8. That's what scripture says, my friend.

Do you have questions? Job did. You see, Job asked at least twenty questions, and guess what? God did not get angry. He gave Job the answers because God had the answers—all of them. He is the answer. After all, He wrote the book. In fact, He lived the book. He is the living Word. Be not afraid to lean on the everlasting arms of your Father. He will hold you and never let you go!

The Father of Everlasting Arms

I am the Father of Everlasting Arms, Lean on Me.
I am the Father of Everlasting Arms, Lean back on Me.
Lean on Me, Lean on Me, and I'll hold you, my child.
When the storms of life engulf you, Lean on Me.
When the storms of life engulf you, Lean back on Me.
When your friends all desert you, Lean on Me.
When your friends all desert you, Lean back on Me.
When sickness overtakes you, Lean on Me.
When sickness overtakes you, Lean back on Me.
When you feel broken and forsaken, Lean on Me.
When you feel broken and forsaken, Lean back on Me.
When there is no one to turn to, Lean on Me.
When there is no one to turn to, Lean back on Me.

When this life is almost over, Lean on Me.
When this life is almost over, Lean back on Me.
Yes, because I am the Father of Everlasting Arms, Lean on Me.
I am the Father or Everlasting Arms, Lean back on Me.
Lean on Me, Lean on Me, and I'll hold you, my child.
Lean on Me, Lean on Me, and I'll hold you, my child.

I am going to tell you the truth; He can hold you up. There are times in life when friends fail us or mislead us. Husbands sometimes don't understand us. It is in that tender time of grace where God—your Father, Teacher, and Friend—is calling you to draw close to Him and to let Him make you whole. You see, in the end, He alone suffices and He alone is what matters. Let Him love you. God's word says,

> *Come to me all you who labor and are heavy laden, and I will give you rest. Take my yoke upon you and learn from me; for I am gentle and lowly in heart, and you will find rest for your souls. For my yoke is easy, and my burden is light.* (Matt.11:28–30)

Are you tired, my sister? Are you weary, my friend? Do you feel like you are spinning your wheels in this life and all you seem to be getting is dizzy? If so, then call upon the name of the Lord Jesus. Take His Holy hand and go with Him back to your Catholic faith. Go to confession, get right with God, get right with others, and get right with yourself. All of us need the grace of the sacraments to walk the path home to our Savior, Jesus Christ, our Lord and our God on this earth. Can you hear the sound of the Spirit and the bride of Christ say "*Come*"? Listen with your heart. Hear your Father say "I love you!" God loves you with an everlasting love.

Are you empty, sisters? He will feed your soul. Let God fill you with His agape love! The Jesus you met as a child is the same yesterday, today, and forever. Take His hand. He loves you and He feeds your soul. Jesus Himself said, "*Whoever eats my flesh and drinks my blood remains in me and I in him*" (John 6:56). His word is true—that is how much he loves you. I am assured that we in the Catholic Church have the fullness of the truth. This is my testimony and why I believe as I do!

During prayer time one morning, I came across a book I had put in my prayer bag to read. In fact, the author was Teresa Harper, a parishioner at the Church of the Most Holy Trinity at which I was attending at the time. Teresa left this world too soon for all of us but will always be remembered for the many ways she used her gifts to build up our Holy Trinity parish. As I opened the book, I noticed a note signed, "Yours in Christ, Teresa Harper, John 6:56." I had never noticed that little note before! You see, I had received the book from a dear friend back in 1996. That was a time in my life when I was running the marathon of raising my seven children. I barely had time to breathe, so I had not taken the time to pause and read.

Knowing how God works in my life, I decided to look up that scripture verse. As I opened my Bible, I read,

> *He who eats my flesh and drinks my blood has eternal life… For my flesh is food indeed, and my blood is drink indeed. He who eats my flesh and drinks my blood abides in me, and I in him. (John 6:54–56)*

I was taken aback, as I always am, when the spirit of God moves in my heart. You see, only God could have known I had been asking Him to help me truly know that the Eucharist is the real presence of the Lord Jesus—body and blood, soul, and divinity. I believed it was, of course; I am a "cradle Catholic." For those who are converts, that means I was baptized into the Catholic faith as an infant.

Now, how many people realize there is a difference between *believing* and *knowing*? When I was a child, I believed God was real. I *believed* by faith. In my twenties, God began to reveal Himself to me. Then I *knew* He was real. The scripture *"Blessed are your eyes for they see, and your ears, for they hear"* (Matt.13:16) became a reality in my life. Jesus also said, *"Blessed are those who have not seen and yet believe"* (John 20:29). God says in His word, *"When you look for me, you will find me. Yes, when you seek me with all your heart"* (Jer. 29:13). I was seeking God.

To my amazement and thankful heart, God used my sister Teresa, who was now truly His in Christ, to encourage me in my faith. What Teresa Harper wrote to me in 1996 was an answer to my prayer on January 26, 2010. The answer I had been seeking with my whole heart came through that dear friend in Christ, just two days before I went to speak at the church where her husband Bill works. God's timing is always perfect. I guess that is why He is God, and we are not.

To me, it was a direct answer from my Father God who lives and reigns forever and ever. Not only is our Savior Jesus Christ alive in the bread and in the wine, but He is also alive in His word. Yes, my friend, we serve a living God who was and is and is to come. Oh, what a treasure we have in our Catholic faith! Do not be afraid to ask your

Father questions. I am going to tell you a secret. He has the answers! He wrote the Book! God says in His living Word, "*Proclaim His Marvelous Deeds to all the Nations*" (Ps. 96:3). That is just what I am going to do!

Do you believe the truths of our faith? In order to live our Catholic faith, we must believe it. God says, "*Seek and ye shall find.*" If you have questions and doubts, I suggest you to

1. speak with a priest;
2. get a spiritual director or a "Titus II" woman to meet with frequently;
3. join an RCIA program (every Catholic should); and
4. pray and seek—asking questions is good, but getting answers is better!

My husband, Patrick, is a deacon in the Catholic Church. In the ordination to the diaconate, the bishop gives to the newly ordained deacon a book of the Gospels while saying "Believe what you read, teach what you believe, and practice what you teach." What an awesome message for us all! Get to know God, know His Word, know Your Catholic faith, know Jesus in the Eucharist, and have His life in you!

Why did I begin this book with a call to know God? It is because *4 for the Mountaintop* is written for Catholic Christian believers. A believer is one who believes. In order to go to the mountaintop with God, you must believe that He is. I must add that He rewards those who diligently seek Him. "*For whoever would draw near to God must believe that he exists and that he rewards those who seek him,*" we read in Hebrews 11:7.

As we seek His face each day of our lives, we get to know Him more and more. He first becomes our Savior, then our Brother, and one day, hopefully, our Friend. He is our Healer when we are hurting in body or in soul. He is our Father who holds us with His strong everlasting arms. In coming to know and love Him, I pray you will make Him Lord of your heart and your life. We can do a lot of good things in life, but God calls us to do "God things." Daily surrender to His will and daily examination of your conscience will aid you in making Jesus Lord of your life each day.

When you love someone, you want to give your whole heart to them, not just a part of it. You don't hold back or count the costs after you have initially met the one who made you, loves you, and died for you. Keep seeking with your whole heart, and you will find Him. There is always more to know of Jesus.

So do you know God? How can you know God for yourself? Faith comes by hearing and hearing by the word. The word of God also says, "*You will seek me, and you will find me when you seek me with you whole heart.*" Has anyone ever played hide-and-seek with their children or grandchildren? If you are playing with a four-year-old or under, as soon as they hide, they want you to find them. They might say "Here I am, Nana, Nana, here I am!" when they want to be found. Jesus wants us to find Him too. He wants to pop out and say, "*Here I am!*" When we embrace our faith and realize that He is who He says He is, our faith travels from our head to our hearts; it is then that we desire to live for Him alone! The Bible is no longer words on a page but, rather, our God speaking to us who believe.

Jesus is God's gift to us. Our lives are to be our thank-you gifts back to God in response to His unfailing love. Let's see how some Bible characters lived that out. God had a purpose for each Bible character. We can learn from their example and also from the example of the saints.

Men in the Bible Who Knew God

1. *David.* In David's story, we can see his character develop and transformation by the hand of God. David was affectionately called "a man after God's own heart"; although after reading his story, you might be surprised! Today his life would definitely make a juicy reality show or at least the best-seller list. Hopefully none of us in the room would tune in or read about it.

   Although David was a great sinner, a mortal sinner, he knew that He served not only a holy but also a merciful God. When David was weak, he knew that his God was strong. David knew where to go to get the grace need to be strengthened—that is, of course was in God's presence. David sinned big, but he sought his bigger God with his whole heart. He repented, prayed, sang, and danced before his Heavenly Father. He poured out his whole heart to God, and most of all, he trusted and depended on God for everything.

   David found his God to be faithful and true. David knew God, not just knew about God; and because of his personal relationship with God, he was able to praise God from His heart. David did not just go thru the motions; he had a living faith in a living God. David's heart was set on God, and because of his character, God was able to use David. The purpose of David's life was to be king.

2. *Abraham.* Abraham went from childless to the father of many nations with a little help from his wife, Sarah. She laughed when God told her husband that she would bear a child in her nineties. Whenever I read her story, I still laugh. Watch what you pray for. God's ways are not our ways. Abraham was fearfully and wonderfully made! God had a purpose for Abraham's life, to be the father of many nations.

3. *Joseph.* Joseph was favored by his dad Jacob. What did his daddy give him to show his love? A coat of many colors! What did his brothers get? Jealous! Joseph went from "bragging brother" to the man with the most brotherly love. God doesn't always change our circumstance, but truly He changes our hearts along the way. He never departed from Joseph, whether he was at the right hand of the king or given an unjust jail sentence. You might say that "in this world we have much tribulation, but our God delivers us out of it all." Joseph lived out that scripture.

   God raised him up to be the right-hand man to the pharaoh, where he was able to provide for his family during the famine. God put him in the right place at the right time, with a small detour by way of a prison cell. Joseph was fearfully and wonderfully made! God had a plan for Joseph's life. He was betrayed by his brothers but used by God to then save Egypt, his father, and the whole family from famine.

4. *Jonah.* Jonah was a prophet. When God spoke His word to him, Jonah thought that he had a better plan than God. Where did it get Jonah? He found himself in the belly of a fish. I think Jonah would attest to the fact that it was not a "whale of a good time." Ask him when you get to heaven how it feels to be spewed out of the mouth of a whale. Jonah had a change of heart and then obeyed God. When Jonah spoke to the people of Nineveh, they listened and repented. Then God had a change of heart too. He did not destroy the people of Nineveh. Jonah was fearfully and wonderfully made! God had a plan for his life.

5. *Joseph.* Joseph was a gentle giant of a man. He was called to be the foster father of Jesus, God's Son. His role was to protect, provide, and be the head of the holy family. He was Mary's husband in every way except physically. Mary was a virgin. Joseph had the fruit of self-control. God chose a man who could parent His Son on this earth. Joseph proved trustworthy. Joseph was fearfully and wonderfully made! God had purpose for Joseph's life.

6. *Peter.* Although Peter walked and talked with Jesus daily, when his friend Jesus needed him most, he ran away. Yet Peter went from being a disciple who was too afraid to stand alone for Jesus to be the first pope. His name was changed from Simon, to Peter, and to Peter the Rock. It was upon that rock that God built our church, the one holy, apostolic Catholic Church. He may have run away in the early days, but the rock was a firm foundation which holds true to the faith until this day. God was faithful even when Peter was not. Peter was fearfully and wonderfully made! God had a purpose for Peter's life. God had a plan for each woman in the Bible too.

Women in the Bible Who Knew God

1. *Hannah.* Hannah wept from the depths of her soul for a child. Her prayer was answered. She birthed a bouncing baby boy named Samuel. God fulfilled her heart's desire, but her prayer answer came at a price. Once Hannah weaned her son Samuel, she gave him back to God as she promised. Samuel was to be a great prophet and priest. Samuel was raised by the priest Eli, who also taught him the faith. Hannah's sacrifice of giving her son back to God won souls to the kingdom of God. Hannah was fearfully and wonderfully made! God had a purpose for Hannah's life, birthing and raising the prophet and judge Samuel, who would anoint the first kings of Israel, Saul and David.

2. *Mary.* Mary's "yes of surrender" to God opened her womb to house the Savior of the world. His birth brought forth God's plan for redemption. His death brought us life. What life will your surrendered *yes* bring to this world? Mary was fearfully and wonderfully made! God had a purpose for Mary's life, birthing and raising the Savior of the world, Jesus Christ.

3. *Elizabeth.* Mary's cousin Elizabeth, though old in years, brought a young man into the world named John. He became the forerunner of the birth of Christ. His message became the Lenten message for all times: "*Repent for the kingdom of God is at hand.*" Elizabeth was fearfully and wonderfully made! God had a purpose for her life, birthing and raising the forerunner of Jesus Christ, John the Baptist.

Was there purpose to the lives of these Bible characters? Yes, definitely yes! There was purpose, meaning, and there was abundant fruit in each of their lives. Their purpose unfolded as they came to know, love, and serve God. There is purpose to each of our lives too. It is worth the prayer, effort, and surrender needed to get to know God for ourselves. This is good news!

What purpose does God have for your life? Do you know or are you still prayerfully seeking God's plan for your life? He has one that I can assure you. He wants to reveal it to you. "*No eye has seen. No ear has heard, all that God has in store for those who love Him!*" we read in 1 Corinthians 2:9.

Do you see why it is a necessity to know God in order to meet Him at the mountaintop? You see, He is the reason you are going on retreat in the first place. At the transfiguration, Jesus took Peter and James and John to the mountaintop with Him. Did you ever wonder why He did that? I think He wanted to build their faith, to let them get to know Him better, and to cement their relationship as four brothers and four friends. They got to know Jesus in a new way. You can be assured of that. Jesus chose to take Peter, James, and John to the mountain with Him because they were not only three of His disciples but three of His best friends.

Sisters in Christ, if you are not planning on inviting Jesus to go with you to the mountaintop to be with you, you might as well call it a beach trip, a vacation, or just a girl's getaway weekend. I don't doubt that you'll have a ton of fun, but will you come back with a new joy in your heart, a more established faith, or memories that will last a lifetime? Will you come back with just a suntan or a renewed heart? You see, Jesus changes us within as we spend time with Him! We can't change each other. Let's face it, we can barely change ourselves. Only God can change hearts. The heart is a work of God, a work of grace.

So before you pack your bags, get your reservations, or google your trip, invite the Retreat Director, Jesus, to come into your heart. It will be, I promise you, the adventure of a lifetime! Today, sisters, begin by examining your conscience, go to confession, get right with God, get right with others, get right with yourself, and then let Jesus take you to the mountain of our God!

In order to live the quote of St. Francis De Sales "To begin in Love, live in love and end in love," we must know our God who is love; it is then and only then that we can truly love others. He fills us with His love to pour out on all. I guess the Baltimore catechism was right all along—"Why did God make you? God made me to know Him, to love Him, and to serve Him in this world and to be happy with Him forever in the next."

Before I finish this chapter, I want to tell you some good news. God is alive!

O LORD, thou hast searched me and known me! Thou knowest when I sit down and when I rise up; thou discernest my thoughts from afar. Thou searchest out my path and my lying down, and art acquainted with all my ways. Even before a word is on my tongue, lo, O LORD, thou knowest it altogether. Thou dost beset me behind and before, and layest thy hand upon me. Such knowledge is too wonderful for me; it is high, I cannot attain it. Whither shall I go from thy Spirit? Or whither shall I flee from thy presence? If I ascend to heaven, thou art there! If I make my bed in Sheol, thou art there! If I take the wings of the morning and dwell in the uttermost parts of the sea, even there thy hand shall lead me, and thy right hand shall hold me. If I say, "Let only darkness cover me, and the light about me be night," even the darkness is not dark to thee, the night is bright as the day; for darkness is as light with thee. For thou didst form my inward parts, thou didst knit me together in my mother's womb. I praise thee, for thou art fearful and wonderful. Wonderful are thy works! Thou knowest me right well; my frame was not hidden from thee, when I was being made in secret, intricately wrought in the depths of the earth. Thy eyes beheld my unformed substance; in thy book were written, every one of them, the days that were formed for me, when as yet there was none of them. How precious to me are thy thoughts, O God! How vast is the sum of them! If I would count them, they are more than the sand. When I awake, I am still with thee. (Ps.139:1–18)

He is our Savior and also our judge. So get to know Him on this Earth, if you want to live with Him for all eternity! It is never too early or late to begin the journey with Him. Do you hear Jesus knocking on the door of your heart? Do you have room to let Him in?

The Lord Whispers, Listen!

When I was but a little child,
the Lord whispered to me,
"I love you my dear child come closer my child,"
Too busy to hear I went about my day—my way.
As I grew to my teens,

the Lord whispered to me,
"I love you my dear come closer my child."
Again, too busy to hear life passing by, sigh,
when I became an adult,
the Lord whispered to me,
"I love you my dear come closer my child."
And this time I heard—His every word.
My heart began to search for the one who had called
and loved me throughout the years
and I found Him to be very near.
Now I live in Him and He in me.
And I go about my day—His way.
He whispers to me, "I love you, my dear,
come closer my child."
And my reply to Him is always the same.
"I love you my Lord—I'll walk by your side.
So if you hear Him whisper to you this very day,
be sure and listen to what He will say.
His message is simple and love is the way.
My prayer for you is to seek Him this very day.

CHAPTER 4

To Love God

The word of God says, "*If anyone thirsts, let him come to me and drink*" (John 7:37). How thirsty are you? As you run to the living water of God's word to quench your thirst, you will get to know God. Now, I repeat, to know God is to love God because God is love. In the previous chapter, we saw God's definition of *love* in Saint Paul's letter to the Corinthians:

> *If I speak in human and angelic tongues but do not have love, I am a resounding gong or a clashing cymbal. And if I have the gift of prophecy and comprehend all mysteries and all knowledge; if I have all faith so as to move mountains but do not have love, I am nothing. If I give away everything I own, and if I hand my body over so that I may boast but do not have love, I gain nothing. Love is patient, love is kind. It is not jealous [love], is not pompous, it is not inflated, it is not rude, it does not seek its own interests, it is not quick-tempered, it does not brood over injury, it does not rejoice over wrongdoing but rejoices with the truth. It bears all things, believes all things, hopes all things, endures all things. Love never fails. If there are prophecies, they will be brought to nothing; if tongues, they will cease; if knowledge, it will be brought to nothing. For we know partially and we prophesy partially, but when the perfect comes, the partial will pass away. When I was a child, I used to talk as a child, think as a child, reason as a child; when I became a man, I put aside childish*

things. At present we see indistinctly, as in a mirror, but then face to face. At present I know partially; then I shall know fully, as I am fully known. So, faith, hope, love remain, these three; **but the greatest of these is love** *[emphasis mine].* (1 Cor. 13:1–13)

The world describes *love* in a completely different way! God is love, yet many people reject Him, just as they did 2,000 years ago. Even though Jesus tells us that He is the way, truth, and life, people remain stuck in the darkness of sin (cf. John 3:19). But *"God so loved the world that He gave His only son, that whoever believes in Him should not perish but have eternal life,"* we read in John 3:16. The followers of Jesus not only open their hearts to Christ but also try to love as He loves. God's word says, *"Love one another; even as I have loved you… By this all men will know that you are my disciples, if you have love for one another"* (John 13:34–35).

When I was a new Christian, I used to say that all I need is Jesus. I was bold enough to tell people that if Jesus is my only friend, it will be enough. That was when I was young and foolish. As I matured in Christ, I realized not only the importance of Jesus in my life as Savior and Lord but also the importance of the body of Christ. I see each of my brothers and sisters in Christ as "Jesus with skin on." They are sometimes a hug from God, a word of encouragement, a word of wisdom, or a prayer in time of need. Yes, God uses people we meet along the way to confirm His love and build our faith. So, to love God is to love His people. How well do you know God's people? Who are your friends?

There are many Christians nowadays that are anti-church. They feel because they have Jesus, they do not need the church. This saddens my heart greatly; Christ lives in the hearts of His people and His people *are* the Church—we need one another! *"It is Christ in you, the hope for glory,"* we read in Colossians 1:27. If we walk in the light as He is in the light, we have fellowship with one another.

I tell my unchurched friends who consider themselves to be Christian that even scripture tells us of our need for church: *"And let us consider how to stir up one another to love and good works, not neglecting to meet together as is the habit of some, but encouraging one another"* (Heb. 10:24–25). You are a member of a church to give and to be given to, to serve and to be served, to use your gifts and to glean from others' gifts, and to love and to be loved. In our Catholic faith, it is clear—we need the sacraments. The third commandment says, *"Remember the Sabbath day, to keep it holy…the seventh day is a Sabbath to the LORD your God"* (Exod. 20:8, 10). The Bible says, *"For by grace you have been saved through faith; and this is not your own doing, it is the gift of God"* (Eph. 2:8). The Catholic faith teaches that the sacraments are instituted by the Lord Jesus (*Catechism of the Catholic Church*, 1114–1116). The old Baltimore Catechism says that the sacraments were instituted "to give grace" ("Baltimore Catechism," lesson 13). There is no confusion in that. *"By grace are you saved, through faith, not of our self, but a gift from God,"* Ephesians 2:8 reminds us. Grace is amazing! I need grace, and I know where to get it—through the sacraments in the church.

We need God and the body of Christ; we need close, God-filled friendships. Jesus Himself loved all but invested His time in three main people—Peter, James, and John. They were His closest friends. I have found the same true in my life.

Close relationships are people who cry with you when you need a shoulder to cry on and laugh with you when you want to laugh. They are your support system; they, next to your family will—only if you let them—teach you the most about God's love. They will help you to be whole and to be holy. The Book of Sirach says, "As you are so your friends shall be like you." So choose your friends wisely.

I have learned to pray that God will choose my friends for me. He does a better job than I could. Pray, ask Him, and then wait. Choose your friends with prayerful discernment. You will find faithful friends who will love you no matter what. They will pray you through life's ups and downs.

You can love everyone. *"A new commandment I give to you, that you love one another… By this all men will know that you are my disciples, if you have love for one another,"* John 13:34–35 says. The Bible says, *"A friend is a friend at all times, but it is adversity that makes a brother or sister"* (Prov. 17:17). The friends you choose should always point you to Jesus. Remember this: I say if you have to change your whole personality for someone to like you, they are not worth the friendship.

Mr. Rogers says, "I love you just the way you are." Agape friends are friends you can kick your shoes off with, be yourself, and know you are loved. Do you want to have those kinds of friends who show you Jesus's love and call you to know and love God better? Friends you can go to the mountaintop with year after year and always look forward to going back again? Friends who have stood the test of time? Then ask God to pick your friends.

Yes, God knows not only what you want but what you need. Trust Him. I promise if you ask and listen, He will surely answer. A word of caution, my friends, Jesus must always be your *best* friend, as does your husband. Do not make a girlfriend an idol; never let them take the place of your God or your spouse. Nonetheless, girlfriends play a very special role in a woman's life. They are important to God as well. We can see the love of God in the way our friends love us. Choose your friends wisely and prayerfully.

One last word of caution: if you begin a retreat group and year after year it is not bearing good fruit, prayerfully discern if the season is over. "*For a tree is known by its fruit*," Matthew 12:33 says. We want to bear the fruit mentioned in Scripture: "*The fruit of the spirit is love, joy, peace, patience, kindness, generosity, faithfulness, gentleness, self-control*" (Gal. 5:22–23). God expects us to bear fruit in due season. If the group is to flourish and draw all four women toward Christ and Christian maturity, it must bear fruit.

So be teachable women and don't forget to back all decisions with faithful prayer and careful discernment. This "4 for the Mountaintop" retreat is not a walk to Calvary; it should be a time of refreshment and peace, a time to restore, to retreat, and to rest in Jesus. God will always confirm what He is directing us to do. If we seek His face, He will show us the way.

Do you see why it is so important that it be God's choice as to whom you go to the mountaintop with? He wants to set your heart afire with His love and teach you to love one another. If it is His choice and His timing, it will be His best for you. It will be a work of grace. So, pray devoutly, wait patiently, and be diligent.

Through the Eyes of my Savior

Thru the eyes of Jesus, I can see
a whining child as saying,
"Please Love me."
As I hold my little son, I remember the blessing he's become.
And thank the Lord for giving him to Me.

Thru the eyes of Jesus, I can see
a husband's love as God's love for me.
As Christ loved the church,
each day it's my husband's search, to love me as humbly.
Thru the eyes of Jesus, I can see
each person I meet as part of Thee.
Their smile, help, or gentle touch
reminds me you love me much-
because we form Christ's body.

Thru the eyes of Jesus, I can see
each day a chance to serve Him faithfully.
"His kingdom come" His will be done
becomes my plea: "Lord, make me like Thee."

Thru the eyes of Jesus, I can see
a trial as an opportunity to be set free.
My weakness becomes my strength,
and darkness becomes light,
as I walk in the Lord's victory.

Thru the eyes of Jesus, I can see
His love poured out for all on Calvary.
A smile upon His face
as He dies and leaves this place,
forgiving all totally.

Thru the eyes of Jesus, I can see
faith, hope, and love eternally.
A grace poured on believers all
for answering God's call,
as we serve Him righteously.
Look thru the eyes of Jesus, and you too
will see those same eyes looking back at you.

PART 2

Our Journey

CHAPTER 5

The Birth of a Work of Grace

Just like a baby in a mother's womb has a beginning, so each group will have a beginning in the heart of God through prayer. I am going to tell you how our "4 for the Mountaintop" group began. As I said before, this is not meant to be a formula. Your "4 for the Mountaintop" group will be totally different than ours. I can say this with confidence, even though I know you haven't yet begun and I have not even met you. God tells us we are "*wonderfully made; wonderful are your works*" (Ps. 139:14). I guess you could say God coined the term *unique*. Let's make that *uniquely wonderful!*

You and the three friends God has chosen for you to retreat with will become your own story. It will be a uniquely wonderful journey—your journey. It will be an unforgettable adventure of a lifetime. Enjoy the ride; take notes. By this, I mean keep a journal! In looking back, knowing what I know now, I would have kept a journal. The thought never crossed our minds at the time. The memories are definitely worth jotting down! Also, be sure to take pictures. As you can see in the back of this book, we have some doozies! A picture is worth a thousand words, and by the time you pass the age sixty mark, you will be sorry that someone had not recorded those thousand words.

Each of our retreats not only had its own theme guided by the Holy Spirit (our retreat master). Each retreat also had its own special memories. I encourage you all that as you begin the journey, please keep a journal. As the years pass by, you will not forget those special times! The old part is guaranteed, the forgetting optional. Now let's move on to the beginning.

Just as there was a great void when God formed the Earth, there was a void in our four sisters' lives as well. We had Jesus, and we were also in a charismatic covenant community in Augusta, Georgia, called Alleluia. In spite of this, we still experienced a void. We craved sisterhood; we needed women in our lives we could trust to be there, to pray with, and to support each other. Relationships are not instantly made, especially with women. Good, godly relationships take a lot of time.

Knowing this, our "4 for the Mountaintop" group began as a social group for suburban wives. Debbie and Pat were best friends; they lived in Aiken, South Carolina. Anne and I were best friends; we lived in the same neighborhood in Augusta, Georgia. Debbie and I both moved here from Gainesville, Florida. I befriended Debbie and gave the invite for the four of us to have lunch together. In our minds, we were just having lunch. God had another plan indeed; we just didn't know it yet. One lunch led to another and quickly grew into a monthly luncheon. This progressed into our "4 for the Mountaintop" retreats.

I do not think our first retreat would have been successful, had we not prepared our friendship with prayer and those monthly luncheons. To be open to another, one must first trust. In order to trust, one must come to know a person well. During those luncheons, we got to know each other. We had girl talk—easy to do since we were all girls as well as young mothers raising children. The girl talk was the easy part. We shared ideas, tips, and advice. Over time, we began to grow in sisterly love and trust each other.

Time passed, and as our families grew, the depth of our conversation grew as well. It grew from girl talk to motherhood talk to spiritual talk. It became a pattern—when we got together, we spent half of our time catching up. The second half of our time, we took turns talking about what God was doing in our lives. To me, that was the best part of our monthly gathering. It is amazing how much you can learn about walking with Christ simply by listening to others whom you love and trust as they talk about their journey with the Lord Jesus.

Sometimes one of us would need prayer. We would stop immediately and pray. Sometimes a sister would share an answer to prayer. Then, of course, we would all praise God with her. We learned to "*rejoice with those who rejoice, weep with those who weep*" (Rom. 12:15). Sometimes a sister would announce that she was expecting a new baby; of course nursing babies were always welcome to dine with us for our luncheons. At the end of our luncheons, we would always hold hands, quiet our hearts, and pray intercession for our needs and the needs of others. We would pray as the Holy Spirit led us in prayer. Each sister would take a turn and pray from her heart. We did not realize in the early days what a moment of grace these luncheons were. God came and joined us for each one! *"For where two or three are gathered in my name, there am I in the midst of them,"* Matthew 18:20 tells us. The four of us lived this verse and can attest that it is true!

We truly looked forward to our luncheons, and as time went on, they became more and more fruitful. I became the facilitator of the group. My role was to call each sister to set up the time and the place to meet. After having it on the calendar almost three weeks in advance, I still would call Anne, Debbie, and Pat the week before to make sure we were still on board. On the day before our luncheon, I would confirm with still another phone call—because life happens! Any mother of many children knows that one.

The job of facilitator is essential. I volunteered because of my ability to be organized and persistent. These are gifts God gave to me, and I used them to make sure this group met and all attended. So someone with those gifts has to step up to the plate or, as we said, "life happens" and the group will fail due to human error. I, the people person, did not mind connecting with my three favorite sisters each month. I thank God I was able to fill that role.

Another essential part of the group was the discernment. Debbie and Pat were quick to tell us when we got into gossip or if they felt a disturbance of peace. "Oh, isn't the sky blue?" became the expression used to change the subject when our conversation got off the mark spiritually. Anne was the discerner to give the hard word; like the prophet Jeremiah, if she felt that her message was from God, she spoke it out unafraid. Pat was the compassionate one, always erring toward love and keeping the peace, making sure no one felt left out or offended, even if it was someone at another table. Pat and I, who never met a stranger, kept our luncheons from ever getting boring by meeting all kinds of interesting people along the way. Each luncheon was as unique as we were. It was no surprise to Anne or Debbie if I was found exchanging names and numbers with another customer in the restaurant because I am a networker. Many times, Pat would leave another customer by saying, "We'll pray for you all." The stranger was always blessed, and so were we!

After years of once-a-month committed blocks of time together, Anne suggested a retreat in the mountains of North Carolina at her parents' home. The vote was unanimous; we all agreed to spend a weekend there together. Now it was time for the facilitator, me, to take action! It was worth the many phone calls and calendar checks finding a weekend where we could all take off!

Anne's parents lived in an exquisitely decorated beautiful home. It was also very quiet and secluded. We barely noticed that her parents were there during our weekend. After all, it was their home! It was on this first retreat to the mountains in North Carolina that God cemented our four hearts together forever. Yes, as we look back on the thirty-plus-year span of retreat, we have to boast that it was all grace. It was definitely a work of the universal God on that winter weekend in North Carolina. There, our "4 for the Mountaintop" retreats were born. God gave birth to it, as He gave birth to all the great things in creation. That weekend, God had created a band of sisters bonded to each other in Christ for life.

Today, I sit at the beach in Florida while I proofread the book *4 for the Mountaintop*. I hear the Holy Spirit say, "*Call for prayer before you proofread, please.*" I know just who to call, Debbie, who not only has a gift for intercession but also a well-worded tongue. I know her prayer will provide the anointing of grace I need to bring this book to the finish line. I know that Debbie will be the least of the chit-chatterers, and even though I love to chat, I am time marking today.

I get Debbie right away; she prays, and we catch up on each other's lives in record time. I tell Debbie that I am at the ocean. Since Debbie and I are the Florida girls, we share a love for the ocean. She and I rejoice and laugh together that our "4 for the Mountaintop" retreats take place almost always at the beach, where there are no mountaintops at all. We sometimes do not even catch a cool breeze, only the wind of the Spirit carrying the four of us to the mountaintop of God. This is the mountaintop we climb together, year after year.

As we go away together with our Jesus, Anne, Debbie, and Pat and I can all agree that it has been quite a climb. This is a climb which has taught us to treasure the moments and to enjoy the view. Debbie says goodbye as we both turn off our cell phones; but somehow, I feel that Anne, Debbie, and Pat are with me here at the ocean. I quickly realize that for now, they are here only in my memory. I take a moment to recount some time spent on retreats long past, taking those treasured moments out of the box of yesterday memories with a smile. Coming back to the present, here alone on the beach, I realize God always remains. I immediately thank Him that He is enough. I am not alone after all. He is always with me.

I thank God from the depths of my heart that He has bound us together. Anne, Debbie, and Pat are treasured friends who are there for me no matter what. Even when we are apart from each other, we are near at heart. These three sisters are the ones God handpicked by my Savior Jesus Christ to be my "4 for the Mountaintop" retreat sisters. This journey has been a work of grace accomplished by God from the very beginning. None of us can take credit for any of it.

As the ocean waves crest on the edge of the sandy beach and the breeze of the wind blows my notebook papers to and fro, I quietly thank Jesus for my three friends Anne, Debbie, and Pat; and then I applaud God. I picture in my mind's eye my Heavenly Father smiling down from heaven. I know that His arms of everlasting love are around me. As I listen with my heart, I hear Him proclaim to my soul, "*What no eye has seen, nor ear heard, nor the heart of man conceived, what God has prepared for those who love him*" (1 Cor. 2:9). I somehow know that He is instructing me to pass this work of grace and truth down to the next generation. Jesus said, "*For this I was born, and for this I have come into the world, to bear witness to the truth*" (John 18:37).

God has called me to build sisterhood, to educate women in the faith, and to be a "Titus II" woman. I know He alone is my source. All of a sudden, time stands still. For once I am speechless. It is a miracle because God has the last word. His anointing is placed on the pages of this book. Through the eyes of faith, I know that this book will bear good fruit for those who read it, if they call upon God's Holy Spirit to teach them. I pray that each reader will seek God's face and grow closer to Him through the pages of this book. I pray that your ears will be open to hear the voice of God's Holy Spirit in your heart. "*But blessed are your eyes for they see and your ears for they hear*," we read in Matthew 13:16.

I thank God for His great love. Jesus died for all of us; that's how much He loves us. My desire is that we all surrender to Jesus as Lord and live for Him. Do you hear Him calling? Remember, the best is yet to come!

Now right on the beach, I break into song, "I Surrender All." I sing, "I surrender all, all to Jesus I surrender, I surrender all." I do feel like Maria von Trapp from *The Sound of Music*, I think to myself. Maria also climbed every mountain that came in her path.

Sisters in Christ, I want to tell you it is worth the climb! It is worth the climb to get to know God, to grow to love God, and to learn to serve God. If we follow Him, we will be happy one day in heaven with Him. I'll meet you there; together we are all on the journey into the heart of Jesus.

My Heart Speaks

"What do you desire of me?" I asked my Lord one day.
I don't really know what I expected Him to say!
"All I want is your love, son,
"and you and I to be one!"
was His reply.

"I'll give you my money, 10% a week,
"and everything I have is yours to keep.
"I'll give you my time, two hours a day,
"and everything I do, I'll do your way,"
I said with a sigh.

Jesus's reply didn't surprise me in the least.
He said, "My son, I've invited you to the banquet feast.
"Rejoice, be merry!
"Your burdens I will carry.
"Give me your heart, my little one!"

"I know I'll move far away,
"and continually I'll pray.
"Read scripture all day long,
"and never be without a song.
"Father, this will show, I'm your son."

Jesus's answer was as stern as can be,
"My son, what is the matter, don't you see?
"All I want you to do
"is to love me as I love you.
"It has to be a message of the heart."

"I think I am beginning to see
"what you have been trying to tell to me.
"It's not my sacrifice or what I can give.
"There's a message of love in the way that I live."

I thought, "I'll make a new start.
"I'll begin by giving my love to you.
"Now we'll be one, instead of two."

"My child, now you understand what I desired all along
"wasn't your time, money, or even a song,
"but rather your love from the heart!"

CHAPTER 6

The Master's Plan
The Nuts and Bolts of the Retreat

As with all works of God, they begin to grow inside you before they ever take their place in this world. Our retreat plan evolved in this same way. Each time we went away for our two yearly retreats toward sisterhood, we came back greatly improved. There was always a spiritual growth that had taken place. We did not notice God working in secret, as He does in the creation of a baby in a mother's womb. Our retreats eventually took on a set order. Before we knew it, it was a true retreat with a master plan. It was the Master's (God the Father's) plan.

Debbie and I definitely live the maxims of "order brings peace" and "prior planning prevents poor performance." We worked hard each time to keep all of us on task. Pat and Anne, our more spontaneous sisters, kept us from becoming too rigid. As a result, even to this day, peace reigns and joy fills all of our hearts at every single retreat. As I said before, every retreat is unique. However, they would not be retreats to us if certain things do not take place. All four of us remind each other in our daily lives that we must continue to bear out the graces we have gained from our "4 for the Mountaintop" retreats.

The most important point of the weekend is that it is God-centered on unity in the Holy Spirit at its peak. "*Behold, how good and pleasant it is when brothers dwell in unity,*" Psalm 133:1 says. I want to remind you again that this is not a formula for giving a retreat. This is just our master plan, personally chosen by the *Master* for the four of us. It fits our personalities, our lifestyles, and our individual faith journey. It has evolved over the years. It did not happen overnight and is not set in cement. Some retreats have been more fruitful than others. I hope that you will prayerfully plan your retreats, let God lead as you follow, and be open. Allow Him to establish your master plan. Our Heavenly Father knows you and your group best. Pray hard, make a plan, and then have a listening ear to let the Holy Spirit lead you up to the mountaintop. I guarantee you won't want to come back down again, although you will have to! God gives grace in order for us to use and share it in the context of our everyday lives.

This is how we execute the master plan:

1. *Heading out.* On Friday, we drive together to our retreat destination. This is always chosen and planned in detail far in advance. The destination is always different.

2. *Friday-night social.* Choose rooms and roommates for the weekend, unpack, and then have social time. This night resembles the once-a-month luncheons. It is an important part of the retreat. The retreat itself begins here. This is where all of us are listening carefully to one another to see who might need prayer for whatever reason. We are making mental notes at this point for what a sister might need—perhaps a word of comfort, a reassuring hug, or a simple smile and a nod of agreement. That is the beauty and grace of knowing each other so well. We are profoundly connected with each other in the Holy Spirit. Think of it as a heart check; it is like going to a spiritual director.

3. *Playtime.* On Saturday, we spend the day in what we call "wasting time." We laugh and play and enjoy each other's company or we go shopping. Many times, we just walk on the beach for exercise. This is followed by breakfast and showers. Then we pack up towels, umbrellas, hats, lotion, food, drink, and each other and head toward the ocean. Yes, we look like tourists or middle-aged beach lovers. It is our huge smiles that give us away. We're on vacation, and out of our faces glows the light of the spirit of joy shining through us. "Let the Sun Shine In" could be our theme song. The sunshine is God's love!

4. *Getting beautiful.* After an entire day of walking, talking, and reconnecting, we dash full speed ahead for the showers. Since we are all girlie girls and since we don't leave our time at the beach until the very last second, this is now the time to "get glamorous" in fast motion. After the first couple of years it, we discovered who the slowpokes were; I'll never tell! All I am going to say is that

this is when my training of having been a stewardess who had to be in the air looking picture perfect at the Miami Airport at 6:00 a.m. comes in handy. By the way, the fast dressers always go last.

I will tell you how to discern the slowpokes—if it is your first retreat, the slowpokes are the ones who say, "Oh, I don't take that long." Then they begin to iron everything they are planning to wear. You then smile and say, "Please, you go first in the shower," with your best "Southern charm." You see, part of this retreat experience is growth in character. All judgmental spirits are kicked off the mountain or you are not growing. Saint Paul says that one should "*lead a life worthy of the calling…with all lowliness and meekness, with patience, forbearing one another in love, eager to maintain the unity of the Spirit in the bond of peace*" (Eph. 4:1–3). This is the retreat theme song.

5. *Confession.* The next stop on our mountain tour retreat is to confession. This has become a favorite and essential part. After the talking, laughing, and sharing time together of the last twenty-four hours, it is now time to quiet our hearts. We've had our showers; we have made ourselves beautiful on the outside. Now is the time to become clean and beautiful on the inside! Together, we march ourselves straight to the arms of our Heavenly Father, where we belong.

   We always try to arrive at the church early, which is a minor miracle in itself, considering our beloved slowpoke! Confession is a highlight for us and almost always ranks among the most-talked-about subjects of the weekend. In the many churches into which God has led us in this over thirty-year journey, each priest has become our favorite confessor. They remain our favorite until the next retreat. One by one we receive the grace through the priest that only God can provide; now we have clean hearts and clean consciences; we are ready for ministry and prayer.

   This humility before the Lord, in putting the sacraments before ministry, opens our hearts to Jesus. Freed from sin and properly nourished, we become ready to be used by Him in ministering to one another. The sacraments are an essential part of this retreat; they create room in one's heart for more of Jesus and less of self. "*He must increase, but I must decrease,*" John 3:30 reminds us.

6. *Adoration and mass.* After confession, we all then begin to look for the adoration chapel. We always count it as a double blessing if we find one at the church we have chosen. Filled with the grace and peace of the sacrament of recon-

ciliation, we continue in prayer until mass starts. No matter what church we choose, you will usually find us in the front pew, singing the entrance hymn with our whole heart, mind, soul, and strength. After all, we are on retreat! It is not that the mass there is better than in our home parish. It is easier to concentrate when we do not have an active toddler, an unhappy teenager sitting next to us, or an overbooked schedule disturbing our thoughts. We are able to focus, so focus we do! We hardly notice when the Mass ends and are usually the last ones out of the church.

Sometimes, especially in these later years, we will ask the priest to pray over us; we ask his blessing on our retreat. It is a powerful moment, and a tremendous grace-filled time follows.

7. *Eat, drink, and be merry.* What follows this? We eat, drink, and be merry physically; and then we eat, drink, and be merry spiritually. It is a banquet of life in Christ. It is a feast—food, fellowship, and godly conversation.

Dinner is always a unanimous decision. All of us discuss and then decide. It is different every time, depending on where we are. Sometimes we eat out; sometimes we eat in. But no matter what, we have lots of fun and love every second of our time together. What always remains the same is the car conversation, which of course always centers on the Lord Jesus. We almost always talk about the priest we met and how confession changed us.

One time, we went to Asheville and had chosen the Biltmore for our "wasting time" part of the day. We decided to go to the wine tasting, just before confession. I am the lightweight of our group who, after one drink (or sometimes even one sip), gets tipsy! Of course, it was on that day I was selected to be first in confession. They all deferred to me—I'm sure they had a good little giggle as I wobbled into the confessional!

Father was excellent; I sat down and confessed my sins, which I luckily had memorized. He told us afterward that he thought we all had way too much fun at confession! We all had told him we were on retreat. He was blessed by us and we were blessed by him.

Besides talking about confession, we also discuss the homily, the church, who we met, and how blessed we felt. Okay, you may say we're weird, and you are right! We are weird for Jesus! This is what happens when you meet Him at the mountaintop. He blesses and gives joy that overflows, a joy that no man can take away. He will bind you together forever. Great things happen when

God mixes with us. Just ask the disciples, Peter, James, and John—better yet, ask Jesus. Maybe He will take you to the Mount of Transfiguration Himself.

8. *Into the quiet.* Finally, dinner is finished, and we all calm down. We return to the place we are staying and gather together in a common area where we can comfortably sit together. We have with us holy water, a blessed candle, our Bible, and a crucifix. We also have tissues at the ready, along with our notebooks and pens. We quiet ourselves in prayer, and we begin to wait on God for direction. Inevitably, someone will say, "I think so and so needs to go first." We never go in the same order. God moves deep within our hearts, and we listen and follow His leadings.

9. *Ministry: Essential part of the retreat.* This is where we minister to one another. We keep silent while the sister who is first shares what she would like prayers for. This is a time of listening to the sister and to God at the same moment. When she is finished sharing, we all pray for her. We pray, we listen, and we wait. Sometimes a word is given to the sister by one of us from the heart of God—a word of advice, a word of correction, a word of encouragement. Sometimes a sister will share a scripture verse from the Bible. Sometimes the sister will just need to cry. Women, how many sisters can you cry with? These are the sisters with whom I can laugh and with whom I can cry.

We do not move on to the next sister until the first sister has peace in her heart and her turn is finished. This is how I see the process—three friends are lowering their sister through the roof to Jesus, just as the men did with the paralytic in the Gospel (cf. Mark 2:1–4). We do not clock watch, we do not judge, and we do not offer our advice. If a sister does not have peace we pray silently while God works on her heart and ours. This time together is a time to let go and let God do what He wills. We must all leave pride behind and sit humbly before Him who alone can change lives and hearts. He knows and loves us better than we know each other and far better than we know ourselves. As we yield our hearts and lives to our Heavenly Father, He changes us from within. All four of us can look back and see clearly how many mountains God has moved in our lives through the "4 for the Mountaintop" retreats.

As the last sister has shared from her heart and the last word is spoken in the love of Christ and the last tear has been cried, four sleepy sisters head for bed. We do not have to worry about remembering what God spoke to and through one another because one diligent, very kindhearted sister takes notes during the ministry. I am never the one because I cannot read my own handwriting!

Heading back. Sleep is sweet, and sleep is short. Before we can all say "Alleluia," the sun has come up; today is now tomorrow, and tomorrow is the day we say goodbye and go home. We all quickly dress and have breakfast together. Hopefully we make the time and are able walk the beach together one last time. If one sister did not receive prayers on Saturday night, it is now her turn to be prayed for in the arms of Jesus. No one gets leftovers; we make sure each sister gets adequate prayer time.

As checkout time approaches, we all begin to pack in hyperspeed. Many hands make light work; and we all help in the process of cleaning, packing, and loading the cars. At the beginning, we all rode together to our retreats. We were all in the South Carolina. There was a short season where we all drove separately. As God would have it, even as I began this book, Anne and I now both live in Florida and Pat and Debbie are both in South Carolina. Now we ride again like the disciples, two by two to the retreats. Our God is good.

Now that bags are packed, our goodbyes are said, and we are all talked out (except for me, of course) we now walk down the mountain, back to our everyday lives. There is a new joy in our hearts, a new established faith, and, yes, memories that will last a lifetime—forever and beyond.

The "4 for the Mountaintop" retreat is neither a formula nor an overly planned activity. It is an experience with our loving God. Every one of our retreats has been different, and so will every one of yours be. The only prerequisite is that you allow God's Spirit to guide you. Only then can you expect miracles, miracles of the heart. No one sees it; but it is involved on the inside, like a child in the womb, growing and forming and created by the hand of God. What a birth it will be—"*Christ in you, the hope for glory*," Colossians 1:27 says. You will begin to know that God changes you from within as you spend time with Him. "4 for the Mountaintop" is a retreat to remember, forever!

Come to Me

Come to me, my little ones.
I've called you to be my sons.
Come and partake.
I have died for your sake.
Come to me, my little ones.

Gather around in love.
Let it be me you're thinking of.
When you eat of the bread,
remember what I said—
"Gather around in love."

Rise up and answer my call.
I'm calling you one and all.
When you drink the cup of wine,
remember you are mine.
Rise up and answer my call.

CHAPTER 7

Let There Be Laughter
The Upside for Ellen

I am a Pollyanna person, or so my husband has nicknamed me, so this chapter is an easy one for me. God once spoke these words to me: "Ellen, you are my sunshine." Of course, I jumped for joy. I found it hard to believe as this was a season where I was sleep deprived. I had a newborn with colic, a two-year-old who had discovered temper tantrums, and a husband who was in family practice residency. I was a new Christian trying desperately to learn God's Word and hear His voice.

He added to the encouragement, "*You let the light of my dear Son Jesus shine through you.*" I was so blessed and so humbled at the same time. I felt the only thing shining through me was mother's milk and a yawn. I smiled, thanking God that I, a tired young mother in my early twenties, could hear the voice of God. I felt like Samuel—"*Here I am Lord, I have come to do your will.*" From that day on, God taught me to look for His Son shining through even the stormiest of days. He also taught me to hear His voice and choose to put on Christ, no matter how I feel. Life is choice, and I choose God!

I spent a few years in Florida, and one of my favorite expression I quote almost daily is "The Son is shining, at least through God's people!" Most people just roll their eyes at me. I try to think the best, saying to myself, "They must not realize I am spelling *son* with an *O*!" We all are empty until we let Him fill us with His Holy Spirit of love. Then we shine for His glory alone. God's Word says, "*If you are going to boast, boast in the Lord*" (1 Cor. 1:31; Jer. 9:24). Here are the upsides of the "4 for the

Mountaintop" retreats for me. I have set aside a chapter for each sister, Anne, Debbie, and Pat. Here are my mountain moments, too precious to ever forget!

Ellen

The benefits of the group to me are having sisters I can know, trust, and count on. They know me and love me, faults and all. We learn from one another, and together are growing closer to Christ and each other. I love being together and having so much fun with my sisters. Jesus is Lord over our retreats!

I have so many favorite memories; if I had to pick one, I must say it was the time we went to Walmart at midnight. It was a "Barbie night." I am the sister who loves to dress up, the girlie girl. One retreat night, I had the idea to dress up for dinner, "Barbie style." Picture this—four middle-aged women on retreat in Hilton Head dressed to the nines, like a Barbie doll but totally modest (picture a Catholic Barbie). I must admit the idea almost did not fly. I was close to being laughed off the island, but all the sisters were good sports.

We dressed in our Barbie clothes with joy and then laughed until our sides hurt. Finally, we went out to eat. Two of the Barbies, Pat and Ellen, who are extroverts, danced to the band music at the restaurant. The band had played the song "To Be." We even shared we were on retreat, and the band announced it. We danced 'til we dropped, laughed 'til we cried, and never forgot the joy we had that night. One sister commented that somehow, someway, God used that experience to change her on the inside. I can definitively say that Barbie night rocks, but Jesus reigns forever and always.

That same weekend, another woman came to our retreat—a handmaiden of the Lord who was gentle, more motherly, and a mother who had known the meaning of how to sit at the foot of the cross. It was our own mother Mary who came to us, on our tenth retreat year. The amazing part is that she came through the only sister who is a convert. Deb, Pat, and I are cradle Catholics, but Anne is a convert who married a cradle Catholic. On that particular retreat, during the time of ministry, at one point, Anne was given the anointing to speak words of healing to another sister. With the great tenderness and compassion of a mother's love, she held the other sister, whispering very gently the very words she needed to hear. It was a holy moment to witness. The sister was open to God's healing love working through Anne.

We all sensed Mary's presence in this holy place. I know this because a few months later, she proclaimed that God had done a deep work in her soul that had filled her with joy. It was evident because over Christmas, even her daughter-in-law noticed the interior change and mentioned it. She said to her daughter-in-law, "Really?" To which the daughter-in-law replied, "It happened on your retreat. You came back different." This sister then thanked us for always standing by her and persevering in prayer.

We all can witness the same. Each of us has had moments of miraculous work in our lives. Jesus is truly Lord over our group. All four of us sisters prayerfully desire to have Jesus as Lord over our daily lives. Our retreat weekends are a time we, as a unit, seek His way, His will, and His Trinity. All of us have grown closer to each other and closer to Jesus. Alleluia!

Jesus's Bride

His love is very real.
I feel like a bride.
Since Jesus came a calling
and walking by my side.

The honeymoon's never over
for me and "The Prince of Peace."
We walk thru life together,
with love that will never cease.

CHAPTER 8

And a Few Tears Too
The Downside for Ellen

If every day were easy-
If things were never wrong,
If all our skies held sunshine, and all our days a song,
If we never had to worry, if we never had to pray,
How would we know the blessings
That come with every day?

—Author unknown

This poem was sent to me by my confirmation sponsor, my Aunt Mary, who lived to be ninety-nine years old. Take note, my sister, suffering helps us to obtain a grateful heart. It is in the rainstorms of life that we seek His face through our tears. This is the downside for me. Let there be laughter and a few tears too. If you are a woman, you will have emotions—yes, tears are like rain to the heart. I was at a retreat recently, and a sweet nun stated, "Tears are prayers your heart cannot put in words." Oh, how beautiful and how true! Flowers cannot grow without water; hearts cannot grow without pain and tears.

Just as life is made up of sunny days filled with joy and dark rainy days filled with tears, so are our retreats.

My friend, there are also gray days in our lives, the "in the middle" days. These are just ordinary days; the sun is not shining and our hearts are not rejoicing, yet we are not wailing in pain and agony either. The ordinary gray days can also be fruitful days. They can be a time to think and not do and to thank for and not miss the moment. Ordinary retreats have cemented our sisterhood. They are a time to waste time together, grow to know each other better, and treasure just being together. No one is in a crisis, and no one is in a blessing season. We just are, and together we rest in Him.

The beauty of our sisterhood is that we all began on the same training ground of the Alleluia Community where we had our formation together as young mothers and young Christians. We were all Catholic. We were suburban housewives with large families, and we all knew Jesus. We were very committed to Christ and had a strong desire to grow in Him. We all loved and trusted each other and were there for each other. Without some of those important characteristics in common, our group would not have stood the test of time.

I think I can say in the early days, feelings sometimes did get hurt, toes got stepped on, feathers were ruffled, and pride did rear its ugly head in all of us. No, the fruit of peace did not always reign on our mountaintop retreats. We did not always err toward love, defer to one another, or keep our mouths free from gossip. Yet in the growing pains, we learned to put on *"compassion, kindness, lowliness, meekness and patience, forbearing one another and, if one has a complaint against another, forgiving each other"* (Col. 3:12–13).

When we did it God's way, we left our retreat with joy and smiles and a skip in our step. When we did it our way, well, our husbands had to minister to our immature hurt feelings. Our husbands, who live with us daily, know most of the time that the other sister had spoken the truth. But let's face it, women, the truth hurts. We eventually learned the truth behind a familiar Alleluia Christian Community cliché—that relationships, especially our "4 for the Mountaintop" relationships, were more important than who was right or wrong. In those days, we would walk away from an argument, thinking we were of course the one who was right and everyone else was wrong or, at least, the sister who brought a word of correction to us was wrong.

If you think about it, growing up in a spiritual family is similar to growing up in a natural family. What four-year-old doesn't say in an argument "No, I was right" or "You were wrong" to his sister? We all have learned that if a person is not willing to receive the words given, we must back off out of love and pray. Good timing is everything, and God is the ultimate changer of hearts. In those early days, pride kept us from being "quick to forgive and ask forgiveness," which is still today a favorite line in our Alleluia covenant.

Over time, we discovered that the order of the retreat weekend was vital to how well it would go. We needed to develop a set pattern for our retreats to facilitate a smooth and fruitful time. Saint Augustine said, "Order brings peace." Creating an order for our retreats allowed those weekends to flow in God's peace. For four women, this was no easy task!

I was the compliant one for a long time. I did not like confrontation and would normally keep quiet to avoid it. I had to learn to do otherwise. It took time to grow and mature, but I did learn to speak out. This change began to take place one weekend when we were in Savannah. It was our "wasting time" together part of the retreat. We came to a sign that said, No Parking but chose to park there anyway. One sister said, "It's Saturday, we won't get a ticket." I pointed out that the sign clearly said No Parking. "Don't worry about it, it's okay," the three said in unison. I, the rule follower, said, "If we get a ticket, I don't want to have to pay it. Something in my spirit says we should not park here." Do you know what happened? You may have guessed it.

We shopped 'til we dropped, then ate at a lovely Irish pub, and then had a great time together. When we arrived back at the car, you guessed it—there was a ticket on the windshield! The sister who owned the car was very sad; the sister who parked there apologized. I, for my part, said in my heart, "Dear God, I told them so!" Fortunately, I was smart enough to not open my mouth (a miracle, if you know me).

One sister suggested that we all pitch in for the ticket like we do for gas. We all agreed, but I told the Lord that next time, I would not go along with the crowd; I would stand for what I believe, even if I stand alone. If you ever feel a check in your spirit, this is the way God uses the Holy Spirit to say no or "Wrong way!" It is a red flag. If it happens, even if your friends don't witness it, listen to the Holy Spirit. He is your GPS; He leads and guides you.

I tell women all the time that if they have not heard that voice of conviction for more than week, they should take it seriously. To me, it is a symptom of a greater problem. The Holy Spirit's job is to convict us of sin. To hear the voice of conviction is to hear the voice of God. The closer you walk toward God, the quicker you are to hear Him and the quicker you are to obey Him.

I am saying this not to throw stones at my retreat sisters but, rather, as a teaching point for those who will embark on a journey to the mountaintop together. The truth is, there have been plenty of times that my retreat sisters Anne, Pat, or Debbie felt the

Holy Spirit warn us with a "No, let's not do that," and most of the time we all obeyed. The Savannah trip was one of those times we did not obey. It cost us some money, but it taught us all some very important lessons—that is, (1) obey the rules and (2) speak out if the Holy Spirit convicts you. Life lessons are worth the journey.

With all that said in my typical wordy way, I will conclude with this: change is inevitable; growth is optional. Growing pains hurt; we have matured as true sisters in the family of God. We learned to be quick to listen, slow to speak, and be slow to anger (cf. James. 1:19).

We learned to complain to God and not our husbands; our relationships were too important. We learned to keep confidence. I say we are like Depends diapers. We hold all things in confidence. We do not leak what happened on the retreat. One another's trust is earned. People will not open up to someone who can't be trusted. Be trustworthy and choose trustworthy retreat sisters. The effort we put into doing things God's way and obeying His word were well worth it.

I say let there be laughter and a few tears too because they transform. It cemented us as sisters in Christ for life. As a Pollyanna, I would say that I would not change a thing, so no downside for me. As in a blood family, we have learned to love and treasure each other, faults and all. Sometimes what we thought was a sister's biggest fault became what God would use to bless us most. It was what we needed, and we did not know it. Listen with your heart to all of whom God puts in your life.

CHAPTER 9

Blessed, Broken, and Poured Out

St. Teresa of Avila says, "*Let nothing disturb you. Let nothing make you afraid. All things are passing. God alone changes us. Patience gains all things. If you have God, you will want for nothing. God alone suffices.*"

It is so amazing that you can go to Mass day after day and then one day God can show you something that has been there all along; that moment of grace can change your life forever. You will never be the same. That is what happened to me one day as Fr. Ring raised the Holy Host, Christ's Body, Soul and Divinity, and then the cup of Christ's precious blood in adoration at daily mass one day. God spoke to me as if from the Last Supper, "*Then He took the bread, said the blessing, broke it, and gave it to them, saying, 'This is my body, which will be given for you; do this in memory of me.' And likewise the cup after they had eaten, saying, 'This cup is the new covenant in my blood, which will be shed for you.'*" I reflected about that sentence. As the days went by, I began to learn a truth about growth in Christ; on the journey to maturity, there is a road called holiness, if you choose it. It is a road that will take you to the very heart of God, if you let Him. "*How narrow the gate and close the way that leads to life. And few ever find it,*" we read in Matthew 7:13–14.

Let's face it, when we first come to give our whole heart to God and embrace our Catholic faith, He blesses us. We walk around with a permanent smile on our face. We are sure we are His favorite because we know without a doubt that God loves us more than anyone else on this earth. We secretly name ourselves "God's Dimple Darling"! We sing out loud, "I am my Beloved's, and He is mine. His banner over me is love."

We are waiting patiently of course for the "coat of many colors" to arrive at our door via UPS from heaven. Yes, at first God blesses us! We are blessed indeed! You see, before God makes us Holy, He makes us whole!

Then after a long season of grace (unmerited favorite) God begins to call us to a deeper walk with Him, better known as maturity. We begin to realize that the Christian walk is not all about me, my way, or being God's Dimple Darling! No, rather, it is about Christ in us as our hope of glory, being robed in His righteous and decreasing in sin, self-righteousness, and pride. If we allow Him, God will accept our surrendered *yes* to break us. It is in this season of testing, trials, and tribulation that we begin to know God for our self. God's Word says in Hosea 2:14, "*Therefore, I will allure her now; I will lead her into the wilderness and speak persuasively to her.*"

The Word also says in Deuteronomy 8:2–3,

> *Remember how for these forty years the LORD, your God, has directed all your journeying in the wilderness, so as to test you by affliction, to know what was in your heart: to keep his commandments, or not. He therefore let you be afflicted with hunger, and then fed you with manna, a food unknown to you and your ancestors, so you might know that it is not by bread alone that people live, but by all that comes forth from the mouth of the LORD.*

I must admit, as a new, committed Catholic Christian, I used to panic when God led me to the desert. I too thought that God had left me alone to die of thirst. I learned to thirst after His Word, the Sacraments, and His wise council. I learned to rest in the adoration chapel instead of in front of the television. I learned that God will never leave me or forsake me. I learned to walk on the water by not just quoting the scriptures but by putting the word of God into action. I have found through maturity that the desert is a place of grace. Our Heavenly Father is the perfect parent whose job is to mold us into the image of His dear Son Jesus. In the Book of Proverbs, it says, "*He will instruct us in the way we should go. He will guide us with His eye upon us.*" We are to learn obedience. We can learn it the easy way or we can learn it the hard way. While in the desert, God will send His people a GPS in the form of the voice of His Holy Spirit. We must, if we are a desert traveler, attune our ear to His voice. The Holy Spirit leads us, He guides us, and He lives inside us. God sends St. Michael and our guardian angel to protect us from all harm. Our job is to listen and to obey.

In the desert God sends us manna, heavenly bread, to feed our souls as we read the Word of God. This is the banquet that God has prepared for us in the desert. He calls each of us to the banquet eating table at one time or another. Psalm 23 reads, "*He prepares us a banquet in the presence of our enemies, our cup overflows.*"

If we be still and know that He is God and seat ourselves at His banquet eating table, we will begin to appreciate that His banner over us is love. We will see the choice foods that He provides, and we will savor the moment. What is on the menu? We may be fed the bread of suffering or the gift of persecution, which may be served to us from our closest friends. Job was served that meal, and so was Jesus. God may dish up a heaping helping of humility. Eat up because I can assure you, it will bear good fruit in due season. It will bear the fruit of character which will last a lifetime.

On the menu there is also the fruit of long suffering if you choose it. Lastly, you could order some pain or some suffering as a side dish. I am talking to those who have matured to the point where they understand that in this world, we will have many tribulations. But God will deliver us out of them all. Those who have walked long enough to know that He is God and we are not. He is our Lord, and we obey out of love for him. We do not tell Him, the Potter, how to mold the vessel. Some people think that if we pray with a certain amount of faith that God will do exactly what we want. I do not read the Gospel that way myself. I read that the way is narrow, and few find it. I read, "*If you want to be my disciple, you must take up your cross and follow me.*" The banquet food is not for everyone because everyone cannot stomach the food.

In the Catholic faith, we are blessed to have the truth of redemptive suffering. In order to understand and grasp this truth, you must let the fire fall in the baptism of suffering. This is the purification fire of God's love. This is found on the highway they call holiness where few ever enter. You see, my brothers and sisters, in Christ, as Janet Erskine Stuart said, "Joy is not the absence of suffering but the presence of God in your heart." As we empty ourselves of sin and flesh, God's Spirit fills us. Yes, to overflowing—if we have room for the new wine of the Holy Spirit. We must buy our new wineskins, purchased by Christ's blood on the cross. We purchase them by daily choosing the life of Christ over flesh and death. Everyone knows that you cannot put new wine in old wineskins.

God is near to the brokenhearted. You feel that you are Job until you open up the Word of God and read Job's story. After you fall on your face in deep repentance, you realize that the suffering that you experience is nothing compared to Job's experience.

When you get to the end of the chapter, you read the Word that Job spoke to God, "*I heard about you from my friends, but now I know you for myself.*"

It is on the road that you will begin to get a glimpse of the meaning of suffering. Suffering is not easy; it is hard. Jesus even prayed, "Lord, if this cup can pass by, it is your will, not mine." As the saying goes, "In great suffering is found great graces."

You reread the Book of Job. As you read it, you quickly see that when Job needed His friends most, even though they were present, he felt all alone. Maybe it was the words they spoke. When he needed a word of encouragement, criticism seemed to flow freely out of the mouth of his friends, hitting Job in the center of His broken heart. My mom would always say, "With friends like that, who need enemies?" Job lost everything—children, home, property, health—and, yes, he felt all alone. The journey you take to the heart of the Father can be a lonely place.

Our Savior Jesus lived that same experience. On the road to Calvary, He was all alone. When disaster strikes, sometimes like Jesus at the cross, we are almost all alone. Not only do we feel all alone; we are actually like Jesus—alone. Our friends are nowhere to be found. Remember this, friend: Jesus is there, and Mary is too. Also, those who have been taught to stand at the foot of the cross will be there. Mother Teresa said, "When you are at the cross, you are so close to Jesus that you can kiss Him."

Do you want to be close to Jesus? Do not be afraid to stand at the foot of the cross. You will find, that is where the grace is. You will discover that even if you feel you are alone, God is closer to you there at the cross than ever before. You will be in good company because Mary is always willing to stand at the cross with one who is suffering. Do not be afraid—call upon Jesus.

Are you carrying a cross in your life that seems too heavy to bear? Are you falling under the weight of it? Are the crosses that you are carrying during this season of your life too sad to mention? Call upon Jesus! Some crosses you bear for the sake of the kingdom you will never forget; they change you forever. In great suffering is found great graces! The fruit will be good if you take hold of the nail-scarred hand of our Savior Jesus and let Him lead you. He will never fail you.

Once rooted in your heart, there will reside a compassion for others who suffer that only God can grow there, if you let Him. Suffering tenders a heart, adding to compassion a seed of understanding. This heartfelt compassion will grow in your heart on the road of suffering, if we are willing to let Jesus break us. "*Unless a grain of wheat falls to the ground and dies, it remains just a grain of wheat; but if it dies, it produces much fruit*," John 12:24 reminds us. Yes, our Savior is looking for willing and obedient hearts to fill with His love. Will you give your surrendered *yes* to Jesus?

John the Baptist said, "*I must decrease, He must increase*" (John 3:30). St. Paul said, "I no longer live but Christ lives in me!" (Gal. 2:20). Many are willing to walk with Jesus in the good times; but how many are willing to walk with Him in the bad times, the times of trial and suffering? Just like the marriage covenant teaches us to stick together in good times and in bad, in sickness and in health, as we walk toward maturity in the Lord, we learn to take up our cross and follow him.

During the time of suffering, we need to be a willing vessel—to be broken like the clay pot, to be molded and fired in the crucible of life. On this journey, we begin to know another side of our God. We learn that He is faithful and that He will walk on the water if He has to, to save us. If our boat is sinking, He will carry us on His back if He has to bring you to a place of safety. He will hold us in the palm of His hand.

We also learn about ourselves, and we learn that we are weak. But in our weakness, He is strong; that we are not only human and need not only Him, but we also need the body of Christ. We learn that grace is unmerited favor, not something we earn. We don't deserve it. We learn that we need Jesus to daily save us from our sin and from ourselves, not one time but over and over again. This mission, my brothers and sisters in Christ, if you decide to take it, will bring you right to the heart of God. You will not self-destruct. I promise that you will learn that "I can do all things thru Christ who strengthens me, but apart from you Lord, I can do nothing." You will learn that "I am nothing, and you are everything." Then God will pour you out to love and serve the body of Christ, both in the church and in the fallen world. You never know where God will lead you.

Many of God's chosen ones took the journey on the road of suffering: Elizabeth was barren. Mary was thought of as unwed, and Ruth was a widow. Noah's wife sailed away from home and had to leave all she knew for a boat ride with a zoo full of animals, three sons, and her husband too. Esther left her people to spend three years at a spa, not a Hebrew kinswoman in sight. Miriam got leprosy, and Tamar was raped. These were God's anointed. These are the women He called to do work. What is God calling you to do? Will you take the journey with Jesus? Let Jesus bless you! Let Jesus break you, and then let Him pour you out to bring the life of Christ to all you meet.

Will it cost you anything? Oh, it will cost you everything! It cost Jesus everything. It cost Mary everything! It cost Job, John the Baptist, Peter, and Paul. It cost Mother Teresa, Pope John Paul II, our modern-day saints, and all the saints before us everything—all their time, all their talent, and all their treasure. What did they receive in return? There is no comparison to the great graces God will bestow on those who love Him. This world has nothing worthwhile to offer those who walk the way of the cross with a Holy God.

On the journey, you learn, as St. Teresa learned, God alone suffices. But, oh, my sisters in Christ, I will be honest with you—it is worth the road trip because it is a journey toward the heart of God. The journey never ends until we come face to face with our Savior in our heavenly home.

I have learned that true virtue does not grow unless it is tested on the path of unbearable suffering and in the crucible of humiliation. Once a seasoned traveler along this path, you will begin to understand with a glimmer of hope the words of Jesus, "*If you want to be my disciple, you must give up, home, mother, father, brother and sister; take up your cross and follow me.*" I have journeyed to mountaintops of great joy, into valleys of tears and sadness, and through deserts of loneliness, waiting until God parts the Red Sea. I have learned that in the crucible of suffering, you get to know God for yourself. He alone will teach you how to walk on the water, if you keep your eyes on Him.

When you begin to sink, He will send a lifeboat in the form of other committed followers. No one can walk the journey alone. I learned, just as St. Teresa of Avila did, "God alone suffices!" Jesus taught me how to put my trust in Him alone. He taught me how to find joy in His presence and how to find wisdom in His word. He taught me how to walk on the water by keeping my eyes on Him. I walked along the desert path, Jesus and me together.

Alone with my Jesus, I walked unafraid. There were times that we would stop to gaze upon a rainbow together. Other times my Jesus would shelter me from a storm under the umbrella of His love. I found joy in the adoration chapel, retreats to the beach, the Mass, confession, spiritual reading, interceding with my prayer partners over the phone, in songs of praise, reading scripture, building and serving family, and sitting at the feet of Jesus in my quiet time. I was lonely for people, but I was held tightly in the palm of my Father's hand.

Unless you have walked the lonely road with the Savior, you will not understand what a grace this was. I was absent from people but present to God. It was in this time of great suffering that great graces were bestowed upon me in abundance. I began almost every daily Mass with my mascara applied to both eyes with the perfection of a makeup artist. By the end of Mass, I found tears streaming down both checks while the mascara decorated my face. I wept for conversion of souls. My soul was at the top of that list. You see, the closer you get to Jesus, the more you realize how much you need a Savior.

Your sins are paraded before you, day and night, constantly reminding you of how much you need Jesus. The price He paid for my sins is no longer just a debt I could not pay but, rather, a demonstration of agape love through His amazing grace. Now I no longer try to win His love, but I am filled with a joy and thanksgiving for what He has done for me. My life has become a thank-you gift to my Abba Daddy who was and who is and who is to come. In Him I live and move and have my being. In grace I fully pour myself out as the hands of Christ to all I meet.

First, of course, I would try to meet the needs of my family and then others. You see, when Jesus fills, you have to pour it out or you will overflow. I wake up every morning to pray and seek the face of Jesus and to take a strong hold of his nail-scarred hand. I listen for His still, small voice and then try to do what He tells me. I know I need Him. In God alone, I place my trust. Sometimes God calls you to walk alone with only Him as your companion.

St. Frances de Sales once said this:

> Do not look forward to what may happen tomorrow, the same everlasting Father who cares for you today, will take care of you every day. Either He will shield you from suffering or He will give you unfailing suffering and He will give you unfailing strength to bear it.

The Word of God says, "Blessed are those who wash their robes to eat from the tree of life" (Rev. 22:13). Invitations have been sent out for the wedding feast of the Lamb. Bride, are you ready? The King is coming! It may be in a day or it may be in one thousand years, no one knows the day or hour He will arrive. What we do know is, we have today to make our hearts ready to receive Him. Let our heart cry, *"Thy Kingdom come, on earth as it is in heaven!"* Let's make our Abba Daddy proud! He gave His all for us; let us give our all to Him. Bless us Lord! Break us, Lord! Pour us out, Lord!

St. Theresa the Little Flower says, "I would like to find an elevator to lift me up to Jesus because I am too little to climb the rough staircases of perfection. The elevator that must lift me up to heaven is your arms, Jesus!"

Is Jesus Enough?

My Father said to me, "They crowned my son Jesus with thorns.
"Is that not enough?
"And you say to me, do I love you?"

My Father said to me, "They mocked and smote my son Jesus.
"Is that not enough?
"And you say to me, do I love you?"

My Father said to me, "I have given you my son Jesus.
"No greater love has no man,
"Than to lay down his life for his brothers.
"Is that not enough?
"And you say to me, do I love you?"

"Know that you are mine, and I love you."

CHAPTER 10

As Plain as the Nose on Your Face

God says, "*Therefore behold, I will allure her, and bring her into the wilderness [desert], and speak tenderly to her*" (Hosea 2:14). In the desert, God can teach you a lesson you will never forget, just like He taught the Israelite people. Hopefully your lesson will not take forty years as it did the Israelites! I suggest you learn at the mountaintop with a little help from your friends. I also suggest you learn by listening to those who love you—your spouse, your children, your parents, your siblings, or your friends. They who are closest to you know you best and are best able to speak the truth in love. If all else fails, learn in the desert. I can promise it will be a lesson you will never forget.

In the desert, my Heavenly Father feeds me the food He knows I need to grow. It is out of His divine love and unending wisdom that He brings you into the desert. Your loved ones or friends may have tried to show you some character trait that needs to change, but your ears blocked the message and your heart was closed to receive it. Picture a kindergartner in an adult body with a finger in each ear, saying, "I cannot hear you!"

You go to the mountain and enter into a time of focused prayer and ministry with your three sisters in Christ. Suddenly, a miracle happens. You not only hear the words of correction, but your heart is open to change. I once saw a bumper sticker that said, "Change is inevitable, maturity is optional." Why did your heart change? It changed because on the mountain, you encountered the God of love, Jesus the Savior. He changed you within as you spent time with Him.

As you go to the mountain, let your cry to God be, "Change my heart, O God, make it ever true. Change my heart, O God, may I be like you." These words of an old song should become the theme song of our Christian journey. My sister, always remember that the change you need is as plain as the nose on your face. You cannot see your nose unless you pull out a mirror. Learn, then, to trust those who clearly see your character day after day. They will become your mirror.

My three mountaintop retreat sisters have been like a mirror to me. They show me just how I look to others. It can become a stumbling block if your heart is closed. It can become a stumbling block if you let pride be your guide, instead of love. It can become a stumbling block if you let anger get in the way and lose trust in those who are trying to help you grow in holiness. Both ears and heart must be open in order to truly receive the wisdom of others.

We must always listen, but then we must carefully discern. Not every voice is of God. "*Beloved, do not believe every spirit, but test the spirits to see whether they are of God; for many false prophets have gone out into the world,*" 1 John 4:1 reminds us. Does what you are hearing give you peace? Have you heard it before but were too stubborn to change? Is the correction given in love? A great prayer to pray before any ministry is this: "Jesus, meek and humble of heart, make my heart like unto thine." This is an old Catholic prayer. The message is profound. It takes humility to give or receive correction. Let's face it, it takes humility to change. Pray for this virtue often in the quiet of your hearts.

The lessons I learned on the mountaintop are many, too many, for one chapter of this book. So I will write about the greatest lesson I learned on the mountaintop. It was a profound experience that opened the eyes of my heart.

As the Pollyanna of the group, I lived under the impression that I never got angry. This impression caused a tendency to be somewhat judgmental of those who lost their cool or had an outburst of anger that I did not see coming. On the very first retreat, God exposed this weakness. It quickly became evident that not only did I become angry, but I buried that anger so deep I could no longer feel it. The downside of this is that anger can only be repressed for so long before it explodes like a volcano shooting volcanic ash at anyone who gets in the way. Yes, it happened, and no, it was not a pretty sight. You see, often it would explode at inappropriate times or at the wrong person. I think it was always the person that inadvertently pushed that one last button. Yes, I would be the person who blew up on the "last button" person because the person I was really angry at was not there. I would sometimes explode at myself. This would feed a depression that was unchecked and not repaired. I was definitely the person who was laughing on the outside and crying on the inside.

Then came the scripture *"Pride goes before destruction, and a haughty spirit before a fall"* (Prov. 16:18). This habit of repressing anger has been an ongoing journey that I have not yet completed. I still have an explosion now and then. I have grown a lot in the wisdom that St. Augustine imparted when he prayed, "Grant, Lord, that I may know myself that I may know You." I have learned to talk to God about my anger or my disappointment. I've learned to forgive in the very moment I have a thought of anger toward a person. I've learned to seek God's forgiveness in the sacrament of reconciliation. I am a frequent penitent. I have learned that instead of saying "that's all right" or "no problem" to keep up the appearance of the compliant, easygoing person, I can now admit to myself and others that it is not okay. I can say, "Yes, I do have a problem with that" or "I am upset about what you said [or did]." This has been a leap of faith and a growth in maturity in my life.

I thought that I was fine holding back my feelings and opinions. Now, I find more freedom in truth. I no longer play a pretend role but live the scripture *"If we walk in the light, as he is in the light, we have fellowship with one another"* (1 John 1:7). I stand now for the truth of God's word, even if I stand alone. When truth reigns in your heart and forgiveness flows, you walk in peace and stability. Depression rarely knocks at my door; if it does, I know how to handle it.

I have even changed my vocabulary. I say words like "I am willing to defer to you, but it will be a sacrifice for me," or "I'll take one for the team," or "No, I cannot agree to that in good conscience."

Lastly, when conflict does arise, instead of immediately taking the blame just to keep the peace, I say, "No, this time it is you. You need to ask my forgiveness. I know you do not like to be corrected, but I will not take the blame if I did not do it." So when I am wrong, I ask forgiveness; but when I am right, I do not bend, especially in the area of sin. I do pray and ask God to change my heart if I am wrong. I go for counsel to an older woman or to a spiritual director. I bend if I can but not if I think it is going to harm me spiritually, mentally, or physically. I had to learn this lesson the hard way.

So has it been a mountaintop experience for me? Yes, but the change has been an uphill battle wrought in prayer on my knees. It has taken a bucket full of grace. Grace has carried me from the weak person I once was into a woman of strength in Christ and His truth. Being a good Christian woman never means to be a doormat!

You see, dear reader, there are supermoms, superwives, or supersisters only in Make-Believe Land. All of us are human. We all have our limits. We all get angry. Anger, I had to learn, is not a sin; it is an emotion. It is an emotion you must learn to deal with in a healthy way, unless you want to be face to face with a volcano. The Word of God says, "*Let every man be quick to hear, slow to speak, slow to anger, for the anger of man does not work the righteousness of God*" (James 1:19–20). This scripture has become a lifetime goal for me. The Word of God also says, "*For God did not give us a spirit of timidity [fear] but a spirit of power and love and self-control*" (2 Tim. 1:7).

I have learned to forgive and to be forgiven, to love and to be loved. I have learned in relationships to give and to be given to. Live in the light and remember the adage "Honesty is the best policy." Now search you heart, my friend, take this chapter to prayer. Ask God if you are holding back negativity. Ask God if you need to forgive anyone. Ask God if someone needs to forgive you. Go to confession and receive the grace to have a change begin in your heart. Where do you need to change?

Find those three "for the mountaintop" sisters whom you trust and listen to them. I say with delight that I would not be who I am today, strong and confident in Christ, without my mountaintop sisters. As I close this chapter, I want to publicly thank my retreat sisters, Anne, Debbie, and Pat. They have accompanied me to the mountaintop year after year. They have been the heart of God to me. This journey has helped us all grow and has made us whole. Thanks be to God! It is as plain as the nose on my face.

CHAPTER 11

From Girlfriends to Sisters in Christ

When I say the word *go*, close your eyes and picture your childhood best girlfriends. Okay, who had that BFF (best friend forever) pass through your mind's eye before you even closed your eyes? Since most women are relationship oriented, we remember forever the good times with the friends. Most of us don't even have to pull out the old photo album or look on the computer folder marked Pictures because those Kodak moments are etched in our memories, with no camera needed.

Surprisingly enough, I was never much of a girlfriend gal before marriage. Moving every year in my youth was not conducive to long-lasting friendship, so girlfriends were few and far between. It was not until high school that I found myself with a BFF. Her name was Sarah. In the short span of high school life, Sarah and I shared experiences that will remain always in our memory banks.

We also shared our wardrobes, our families, and our lives in detail. Sarah and I, now "seniors with life," have lived on different coasts most of our married life; but this distance is shortened by being only a phone call away. Sarah is still one of my first phone calls when life's journey takes me to the valley of despair or to the mountaintop of great joy. Our girl talk immediately takes us back in time to being the two high school girls who knew each other so well, even better than a family member. After all, Sarah was like a sister to me. It seemed that in high school, I always got along with the guys better than the girls. Sarah was really my only girlfriend at that time in my life. Sarah still is BFF—my best friend forever.

4 FOR THE MOUNTAINTOP RETREATS

Once married to my Patrick, I was compelled to explore the world of girlfriends. The woman out there who likes me balked at the idea of a close female confidant in the early years of life and embraced the relationship when they became a mommy. Motherhood is a world all of its own. New moms have questions. Since newborns don't come with directions, many moms are asking the question "What's a mother to do?" Inevitably, the new mother quickly realizes that they need other woman and not just to answer their questions.

In addition to advice and wisdom, they need support. Moms need to walk along with another woman who has the map and who has already done the motherhood journey. Another mom has a way of understanding postpartum depression, nursing a baby, sleepless nights, and colic better than a husband and better than a male physician. You see, moms haven't just read the books on the subjects facing their daily life as a mom or google their problems; moms have lived it. A strong bond begins with the girlfriend with whom we go through the childbearing years that will never be broken.

These girlfriends can discern when we need a day at the spa, when we are sure we need to run away to the Hawaiian Islands and leave behind the forwarding address unknown. These girlfriends will talk for hours on the phone with us to get us through a relationship problem. Even if we say "I'll never speak to that person ever again," our girlfriend never judges us. After a good cry and some heartfelt advice from our best girlfriend, our hurts are washed away; and we always decide that we were overreacting, hormonal or both. A girlfriend has a way of reminding us that the relationship is always more important than who was right or wrong. A girlfriend has a way of reminding us that this too shall pass, in a way that it seems believable. We decide she is right; it almost always does.

Nowadays, my view of girlfriends has changed dramatically—from friends to sisters in Christ. God knew I needed a friend that sticks closer than a brother. The Book of Sirach reminds us, "*A friend is a friend at all times but it in adversity that they become a true sister.*" Over thirty years ago, I began to form a friendship with a group of four women, which we now call "4 for the Mountaintop, of which I am blessed to call my best friends and sisters in Christ. It took a journey."

We began getting together as just a monthly lunch bunch. We found we had a lot in common—all Catholic; all married; all moms of many; and all wanting to know God, love God, and serve God. On our monthly get-togethers, we laughed together, cried together, shared our lives together, and soon shared our hearts. It was not long before someone suggested, "Let's go away together on a retreat." The plan was set in motion in no time at all.

We found ourselves at one gal's mom and dad's mountain house with Jesus as our Retreat Master. It was glorious. At the end of the weekend, just like Peter, James, and John at the transfiguration, none of wanted to come down the mountain. We all knew we had to. The retreats became a refreshment from the everyday routine of life.

At the end of the weekend, we all return to our families with a new skip in our step and a smile on our face that glowed from being with Jesus and true friends.

When my three best girlfriends and I go away on a getaway weekend retreat, rarely do we check our e-mails or watch television until our eyelids close. No. Rather, we shop until we drop, maybe take in a movie, and, of course, we enjoy good food and fine wine. We sit in the sunshine and enjoy the view and always talk until we have no voice left. These are the activities we do for enjoyment. We also feed our souls by going to confession, assisting at mass and sometimes adoration. We pray for and with each person we meet along the weekend—from the waitress who serves us at lunch to the maid who cleans as we leave.

On the last night away, we each take a turn and not only share in-depth what is going on in our lives but also what is going on in our souls. Then we pray for each sister, give practical advice, rejoice in their good news, and sorrow in their sorrows. Girlfriends listen with their heart instead of their ears. Girlfriends are ever ready with a kind caring reply and a Kleenex to wipe our tears away. Besides, girlfriends rarely say "We will talk about it later" because they know some things just can't wait. We "4 for the Mountaintop" sisters are there for each other, through thick and thin, in all ages and stages of life.

As we look back on our over thirty-year journey, our "4 for the Mountaintop" retreats, we have come to realize that they were not only a good idea but, rather, a work of God. I think that all women need three best friends to go with them yearly to the mountain of God to seek His face, rejoice in His love, and rest in His presence. Women need women in their lives who speak the same language and understand with their hearts.

I felt so strongly about our retreats that I was motivated to write this book. *4 for the Mountaintop* about our journey to the mountain. We laugh together when I tell the title because we always go to the beach. We cry together when we look back on our journey because we all know it has been designed by God. We look forward to getting away because it is different. One thing remains the same—God always shows up. The work He does is done on the inside of our hearts where He alone sees. He has done a great work in each of our hearts. We are forever grateful.

Don't get me wrong; there is nothing like a man, especially if your man looks like George Clooney like my guy. However, there are days in a girl's life when a man just will not do. On days like that, you know what to do, ladies—call a girlfriend. If you think about it, sometimes a girl's getaway retreat weekend may even top running away to a Hawaiian island, unless George already booked the flight. In that case, I'll pack My Lai and my bathing suit and not forget the sunscreen. Then I'll bid you all "Aloha"!

I Am!

You say to me, "Use me, Lord."
I say to you, "I AM, I AM!"
You say to me, "How, Lord?"
I say to you, "You'll see, MA'AM!"

Be my legs, be my feet,
be my arms, be my hand.
To everyone that you meet,
in every place, in every land.

I use you daily as you yield,
I use you more than you can see.
Many lives have been healed,
many hearts have turned to me.

Be my ears, be my eyes,
be my mouth, be my heart.
I teach you daily to be wise;
in my plan, you have a part.

Open my eyes, Lord, that I may see.
Open my ears, Lord, that I may hear.
Let me see you working in me
and let me hear you very clear.

You say to me, "Teach me, Lord."
I say to you, "I AM, I AM!"
You say to me, "How, Lord?"
I say to you, "You'll see, MA'AM!"

Seek my will, seek my way,
seek my plan, seek my face.
You will see I'm the Truth and the Way,
and in my plan you have a place.

Know that I'm putting people in your path.
Know that I'm guiding each step you take.
Know that you're delivered from my wrath.
Know that I'm leading each decision you make.

Wash the feet of my saints,
wash the face of my poor,
wash the sins from your heart,
continue to open the door.

Feed my sheep, feed my lambs,
feed my rich, feed my poor.
I'm using you, MA'AM!
Feed on my Word some more.

Thank you, Lord, for hearing the cry of my heart,
thank you, Lord, for using me,
thank you, Lord, that I have a part,
thank you, Lord, for choosing me.

You say to me, "Thank you, Lord,"
I say to you, "I love you, MA'AM!"
You say to me, "How, Lord?"
I say to you, "I AM, I AM!"

Now I have asked each of my "4 for the Mountaintop" sisters to write a chapter in this book, so let's hear from Anne, Debbie, and Pat.

CHAPTER 12

Debbie's Story

MEET DEBBIE'

Hi, I am Debbie, the more private one. I tend to keep my personal life and business to myself. Don't get me wrong, I love people and I was a second grade teacher. You have to have a bit of crazy in you to be with children day in and day out. I didn't start out to be a teacher, as my plan was to stay home and be a mom. After several years, it appeared, we wouldn't have children; so I pursued early childhood classes in college. God didn't forget me! So after 4 children, many grandchildren, four dogs, three cats, and two rabbits later, I taught second grade. As noted, my husband and I meet and were high school sweethearts.

I was born in Detroit, Michigan, and transplanted to the Florida Keys after my parents' divorce. Raised as a Roman Catholic, I went to a Catholic elementary school and then switched to the local public high school. After high school, my husband and I married and attended college together. He began his career as a chemical engineer, and I began mine as a mother. Having fallen away from the church, we decided to return to our Catholic faith after the birth of our first son. We had our first home and the storybook life but still something was missing.

After we experienced a rebirth in our faith, we became involved in our parish. In 1981, we felt called to join a Christian community, Alleluia Community, to help foster our faith in a more real way. We wanted to integrate our faith into our daily life. It is with this Christian community that I met and came to know and love the dear sisters spoken of in this book. These are the friendships of a lifetime.

I met Pat's husband when he came to South Carolina to check out the Christian community. The long and short of the story is they lived with us while they built their new home. We became good friends during they stay. Between us, we squeezed eight children and four adults in a four-bedroom house. It was tight, but we kept our humor and made some memories. Ever the hostess, Ellen invited the girls to get together for lunch. Anne had moved to the same area of Augusta as Ellen, and they were good friends, carpooling and doing things together.

We began as casual friends, having lunch at each other's house or a restaurant. Most of our children were somewhere in school, and the ones who weren't usually played at a friend's house or came along in a highchair. Our conversations were just trying to get to know each other better and discussions of the current events in our lives, the world, or what have you. We always shared a laugh and a good time. Our desire was to get together once a month, but it didn't always happen; we lead full lives and lived in two different cities, though only forty minutes apart. We had our faith in common, and our children attended the same school in Alleluia.

After a couple of years, we decided to go on a retreat at the beach. Our husbands said, "Retreat at the beach? Yeah right!" But on we went to the beach, husband and children left behind. The exception was Anne, as she had a newborn and we brought him along. We all pitched in and helped it go well for her—at least, from my perspective it went well.

Soon we fell into a pattern. We would travel to a location together and laugh and visit and catch up with each other. This would be on a Friday night, so it was all about getting our homes in order to be gone for a couple of days without a major crisis occurring in our absence. Then we set about unwinding.

After we were at our location and settled in; we would visit, talk, laugh, and, in general, relax. Ellen usually likes a plan. If we all know what we are doing, then all our expectations are the same and we have less chance of conflict. We have had our times of conflict and hurt feelings; we are humans. Once the plan shaped up, the day began. Sometimes we would walk the beach, or the woods, or the antique, or fabric, or even a Walmart store. Sometimes we sat by a pool or the beach. It seems we would walk and talk on every trip. We would pair up in twos and visit with one of the women we had not seen in a while. Then after a decent visit, we would shift friends and catch up with the other woman. This was just the flow and pattern we fell into. As women, we connected with each other so we had a feel for where each one was in their life.

Generally, we ate lunch out and finished what we were doing. Because we were all Catholic, we fell into a rhythm—we would go to confession and then Saturday night mass. After mass, we would seek the parish priest and share that we were on retreat and ask for a blessing for our time together. After dinner, we had a time of prayer; we decided not to have a glass of wine until we finished praying for each other. We'd slow down and focus on just one person. Each of us came with our own problems and issues from our life. It could be our past or a present problem. The person would discuss what they wanted prayer for in their life.

We learned a few things quickly. Nobody wants a lecture, and nobody has all the answers. We found it best to listen, then pray, and then speak. In the quiet of praying for the person, we each would listen for God's voice, inspiration, and wisdom. God never fails. God is so faithful, merciful, and loving to each of us.

This brings me to the benefits of our little group.

You might think, *Benefits?* Can there be more benefits than three good friends who listen, laugh, pray, and care about you? Oh yes! We decided early on that our friendship had to be based on Jesus Christ, not the fashion, diet, exercise, weight, or what new was happening in the world. Yes, and trust me on these issues. We had to decide on each one of them because we are women and we live in the world; but back to the benefits. We would make it a point to see how our prayer life was going. Each of us would bring new wisdom and knowledge gained from prayer and insights gained from our lives. Often, we would share a new teaching or book that had helped us in our faith. Frequently we'd share wisdom, tips, and skills to use as we raised our sons and daughters. We'd share training tips for our children and ideas to incorporate into our marriages. We'd encourage each other to be a better wife, spouse, and friend to our husbands.

The best benefit for me was a sense of freedom that was new to me. I have slowly become free from the baggage of my past, the hurts and brokenness of a child from divorced parents. After twenty years of opening myself up to others and to God, I have been delivered and set free to become the woman God created me to be before the wounds of life bound me up. I have grown to love God and my fellow man more and more.

We have had some fun and some sorrow. It's always sad and hard when one of us gets upset. Sometimes we have said something without thinking or been careless with our words. There have been times when one of us will be too blunt and lack discretion. Sometimes one of us is just too fragile or vulnerable to hear a thought. When we share from our hearts the pain we each carry, it's then that we often cry for ourselves and each other. God is always on his throne, and we repair our relationships. Often, we are healed, and the tears are a gift of healing and forgiving.

Is this thing one big spiritual trip? Heavens no! We have done some funny and silly things for grown women with kids in college and grandchildren. Many things are just too personal to share, but I can say we laughed like crazy on a midnight ride to check out a potential boyfriend for one of the women. On impulse, we jumped in a car in our pj's and coats to check out this man. One night, one of the women wanted to highlight her hair, so off we went to Walmart at 1:00 a.m. to find a kit.

So here we are, twenty-plus years later. We live in two different states and no longer have lunches together. All the kids are grown and gone. We have some in college, some are single or married, and one is a nun. We still value our time together, and we are all busy with jobs and husbands and grandchildren. Our goal is to get together once or twice a year. Our spouses see the value of our time together and see the changes we have helped each other make.

Now we pray for our children and our children's children. Now we are the "granny warriors." We work to pass on our love and our faith to our grandchildren. We encourage each other to find new ways to share our faith with the grands who are relevant. We continue to encourage each other with the new situations that come to greet us. Sometimes it's a surprise like a divorce or a death, but whatever comes, we want to be there for each other. If not physically with a hug, it's always spiritually with prayer, prayer, and prayer.

CHAPTER 13

Pat's Story

MEET PAT

I am Pat and considered to be the really friendly one who talks to anyone and who asks the questions no one else wants to ask. Like Debbie, I too was a teacher. I taught special education students in the public school system for years but recently retired. Working with young children is the only place I know where you can act goofy and get away with it! I have been married to Fran for five years, and between us, we have seven children and four grandchildren.

I was born and raised in Greenville, South Carolina, and attended St. Mary's Parish. My cousin Kitty, who is my age, greatly influenced me in my Catholic faith. She had a deep faith as a child and later became a Dominican sister. My grandmother also impacted my spirituality. I remember listening to her pray the rosary aloud in the night whenever I stayed over at her house. I have always had a deep reliance on God, but my faith really became part of my daily life when I was in college. I met other women who were deeply committed to Jesus, and their lives profoundly affected me.

As you already know, "4 for the Mountaintop" sisterhood began in Alleluia Community where we all met. God had a higher plan for us than just mere friendship. We had no idea that he would accomplish so much healing and ministry through us. Our combination of backgrounds, personalities, gifts, and struggles is part of what makes our relationship so special. We fit together like puzzle pieces. I feel so blessed to have such beautiful and holy women as my best friends. Only God can bring people together like this.

My walk with God has deepened so much because of these women and their faith. We have walked and prayed each other through so much, including the deaths of a child and elderly parents, disability, divorce, annulment, out-of-state moves, financial struggles, and all that comes with being a mother. We have a saying, "What happens on retreat, stays on retreat." This means that we hold seriously our code of confidentiality in what we share while together. This trust allows me to be able to open up to Anne, Debbie, and Ellen and receive the ministry I need. This is a precious gift, and I often thank God for it.

It is never easy to open up about your individual weaknesses and sins. These women have always given me acceptance, wisdom, and love in those vulnerable times of exposure. We are more than just friends but devoted sisters in the Lord. We have truly helped each other grow in our faith, and I believe our prayers together are powerful.

In the early years of our group, there was a television commercial for a local hospital that featured three women. There were scenes depicting their lives when they were young women, then mothers, and, finally, older women. They had remained friends through the years. I always hoped that Anne, Ellen, Debbie, and I would be those women. Now we find ourselves in later life with grown children, new extended families, and grandchildren; and we are still together!

It is such a gift to be able to call or text one of these sisters and know that they will listen, pray, and offer wisdom for any problem that I have. In fact, we seem to keep a continuous text stream going that helps us stay connected on an almost daily basis. We laugh, cry, and have fun together. God willing, I look forward to many more years of sisterhood!

CHAPTER 14

Anne's Story

MEET ANNE

God puts the most unlikely people together sometimes! Have you ever noticed that? It reminds me of the scripture that says, *"God uses the simple to confound the wise."* I don't claim to be wise, but He sure has shown me many times that His ways are not my ways! And I just sit in amazement at the things God has done in my life through unusual circumstances and people. Let me tell you about it.

My name is Anne. I grew up in Atlanta, Georgia, the second of five children in my family. We grew up in the Presbyterian church, with a wonderful church family, great Bible teachers, an active youth group, Bible camps, and retreats. I was very active in my church, singing in the choir, playing piano for my Sunday school class, and going to prayer meetings and small group Bible studies. I attended public school all twelve years.

I tried choosing my friends in grade school by all the things I perceived as important—good looks, brains, popularity, family status, wit, or whatever makes someone attractive. But I never really felt accepted by those chosen people. I was not a part of the "in crowd," as we used to call that select group. It was only by God's love and mercy that I was able to overcome that sense of inferiority.

It was the summer I was sixteen when I first realized that God loved me just the way I am and felt like He actually thought I was beautiful and worthy of being loved. That's not to say I never struggled with rejection ever again. Over time I learned to recognize that the *fear* of being rejected was the devil's favorite way of attacking me and making me feel unloved.

When my husband and I moved to Augusta, Georgia, in 1990; there were many wonderful people to get to know. In our neighborhood, there were many strong Christian families. Many of the mothers stayed home to raise their children. One woman in particular caught my attention. She had five children, many the same ages as my own children. We, however, were complete opposites!

Ellen was a fast-talking Italian raised in the north. She was a very creative and fun mother who ran her home like a nursery school. There was story time, game time, music time, and, of course, snack time! My kids loved going to "Aunt Ellen's" house because she had the largest assortment of snacks, especially candy, that they had ever seen! And if they were there when five o'clock rolled around, they were expected to take part in cleanup time.

Everything she did was organized, in a good way. She epitomized the saying "Order brings peace." I admired her greatly, even though we had very different personalities. Ellen and I were part of a Christian community called the Alleluia Community. It was a group of three-hundred-plus Christian families in the Augusta area who chose to live out the Gospel teachings from the Acts of the Apostles. The families all met regularly for praise and worship, sharing each other's burdens and joys, being supportive of one another as we all strove to deepen our walk with the Lord.

There were two women in Alleluia Community who were living in Aiken, South Carolina. We arranged to have lunch together with these two women. Pat and Debbie were also best friends and polar opposites. Debbie had been raised on the beaches of the Florida Keys, in a very laid-back and casual atmosphere. Pat, on the other hand, was raised in Greenville, South Carolina, in a more proper—sometimes pretentious—Southern tradition, as I was in Atlanta. Despite our different cultures and upbringing, we each had a desire to go deeper in our relationship as women and mothers. So we began to meet monthly over lunch to share our lives with one another.

We quickly realized that no matter what your heritage or where you were raised, all women struggle with similar issues. Initially, we shared our struggles with children, husbands, in-laws, or our own siblings. We helped each other see the problem with new eyes and a fresh or different perspective. Having opposite personalities can be a blessing in that way. It can open our eyes and heart to how someone else may perceive the situation and be affected by it. We would end our lunch with a quick prayer for one another and the challenges we were facing. Then Ellen, the bold and outspoken one, would usually ask our waiter or waitress if they had anything they wanted prayer for. That is a ministry she still continues to this day. It truly makes people feel loved and cared for (even by strangers). Many people are hurting and feel all alone in their grief. They have no one to turn to who can share their burden. Most say they've never been asked that question before by a customer.

After a couple years of lunchtime meetings, we wanted our ministry time to be more extensive. We decided to try and get away for a weekend together, away from kids and responsibilities of the home. By this time, we had twenty children between the four of us, ranging in age from seventeen to two! Our wonderful husbands reluctantly agreed to let us escape for the weekend, and off we went to the mountains for a wonderful time of refreshment and rejuvenation in the Lord.

We talked for hours, late into the night. We woke up and talked some more, we prayed with each other, sang praise songs, and laughed until we cried. We would take a break from serious prayer to walk around the small mountain town or climb to the top of the mountain to take in God's magnificent creation. On Saturday afternoon, we would go to confession at the nearest Catholic church, followed by Mass. We would ask the priest to pray over us for our retreat, our relationships, and our families.

Our years of lunch ministry had laid the groundwork for trust in our relationships, and we were able to really bare our souls during our times of ministry on those weekends. Having the gifts of the Holy Spirit operating in our lives, we were able to listen for the Lord's words of wisdom and insight. Sometimes it came in the form of a word of knowledge for one sister or a word of encouragement or comfort for another sister.

The Lord would meet us and show us His mercy and love in a very real way. It was a time of great healing for each one of us. It was so good that we decided to go on our retreat twice a year—only the second one would be at the beach in the summer. Definitely another place we see God's handiwork and can relax in the company of loving sisters.

The past over thirty years of retreats have brought tremendous healing to my wounded soul. Through the love and support of my retreat sisters, I have been able to overcome many obstacles in my life. I've been able to forgive those who have caused me pain and sought forgiveness for the pain I've caused others. I've grown in my understanding of how other people can suffer greatly in silence and how I can be a strong shoulder to lean on or a gentle embrace to bring comfort. I was given the privilege of caring for my parents as they were getting feeble and suffering in their last years. God used that to bring much healing and restoration in my relationship with them from wounds of my childhood.

I was able to pray with them nightly and sing songs of joy and comfort to my mother as she was bedridden and unable to speak. I could not have gone through that without the daily support of these three precious sisters who know me and have shared all my heartaches and struggles. And yet they love me with the love of the Lord. God has given each of us an irreplaceable and priceless gift of sisterhood that has stood the test of time. We are forever grateful for this gift and encourage other women to seek out like-minded Christian women to build a lasting relationship with and share in their journey.

CHAPTER 15

To Serve God

Any military soldier will tell you that "they train you up and then they send you out." It is the same in the army of God. "God's got an army, they're marching through the land. Deliverance is their song, there is healing in their hands"—these are the words of an old song that I sing often in the quiet of my heart.

In the army of God, just like in the military, there are no lone rangers; soldiers need someone to cover their backs, to hold them when they hurt, and to listen to their stories. Healing comes in a person's heart when a word of wisdom is spoken in love or an encouraging word tells another they understand. Sometimes the words are said in correction and sometimes in agreement but always in love. Sometimes, as a priest told me, deliverance comes through the sacrament of a repentant confession; a sister that points you to the sacraments is a true sister indeed.

As a teenager I spent most of my time with the male sex, with the exception of my forever friend Sarah. It was not until I became a mom that I realized women need women. Why? If any of you have ever read the book *Men Are from Mars, Women Are from Venus*, you will know that once married, we should not be pouring our heart out to or spending our time with the opposite sex; it is a dangerous temptation. That is why the Book of Titus addresses women and men the way it does. My nuns would say, "Avoid the near occasion of sin" or "do not put yourself in the path of temptation." It is dangerous. Why do I say this? Because once married, I had to find relationships and friendships with women, to share, to care, and to waste time with. It was a wonderful discovery. Women *get* women. They understand. So when I joined Alleluia Community, I prayed as I always do for God to pick my friends, my girlfriends.

God did a great job by choosing Anne, Debbie, and Pat. They are the best friends a girl could ever have next to Jesus of course, and my husband Deacon Patrick. These three "4 for the Mountaintop" retreat sisters, over the last twenty-five years, have brought Christ into my life and changed my life.

I applaud God for being a part of it—this foursome—as we look back on the years and see how much we all have changed and grown and how much we love one another with a sisterly love. We all agree, "It is a work of God." We have come to know God better and to love God more.

He has trained us up now. He sends out as His little soldiers to serve Jesus, our Lord and King, and to teach other women what God has taught us. We all feel that this gift of retreating to the mountaintop is not only for us. That would be selfish. It is for the entire body of Christ. I, the author of the group, have written this to teach other women the *how*, *what*, *why*, and *when* of these retreats. Each of my retreat sisters added chapters of their own. I am also a Catholic Christian speaker. I am willing to speak at your church or Christian community, along with Anne, Debbie, and Pat, if they are available.

We can give a morning mini retreat talk or speak at a woman's club or TV or radio group.

CHAPTER 16

Fashioned by God

How many of you have felt called to go to the mission field? I sure did until I discovered they had animals. Father told me, "Ellen, *no* animals." I think he heard me wrong because we all know that priest cannot lie. Then the second obstacle came with the wardrobe. What would I wear? Do heel work for missionaries? As you can see, I am what is called "missionary challenged." I was so sad to discover that the mission field was not my gift, when a miracle happened. Yes, my brothers and sisters in Christ, miracles happen and the greatest miracles happen in your heart.

I come to you today to bring you tidings of great Joy—"good news." I love good news. How about you? The good news is, "Today the entire world is a mission field." Yes, hearts everywhere are longing for the Good News of Christ to come into their fields. However, *"the harvest is ripe but the workers are few."* All of us are given the opportunity to be a missionary right where we are, in our little corner of the world. We are called to be ambassadors for Christ, living the Good News and preach the Good News. St Francis is quoted as saying, "Preach the gospel wherever you may go and when necessary use words."

My friend, in the world today, where the dark is getting darker and the light of Christ is shining brighter, I find words very necessary. We must speak out for the truth of our one holy, apostolic Catholic faith or who will? In order to make a difference, we must know the *how*, *what*, *where*, and *why* of our gifts. So how do I discover my gifts? In order to know your God-given gifts, you must first get to know God. We are all searching. Let me tell you my story.

I can answer questions over the phone as well. In every ta[...]
"To know Him is to love Him, to serve Him and be happy with [...]
is the way we retreat sisters are willing to serve God—by encouragi[...]
retreat group and answer all questions. Your "4 for the Mountaintop"[...]
look anything like ours, but these at least are guidelines to help begin [...]
It will be a road trip that you will never forget. Don't forget to take your [...]
Power— working through his holy—Spirit). You will have the adventure of a l[...]

You will discover that the "*eye has not seen nor ear heard what God has in sto[...] those who love Him*" (1 Cor. 2:9). We've found this to be true. Jesus will always be o[...] best friend. And of course, our wonderful husbands will be our soul mates, lovers, and [...] best friends. But oh the retreat sisters that God has called together! If you ask Him for His choice of three others—sisters to run with who will become the sisters that God talks about in Proverbs 17:17: "*A friend is a friend at all times but it is adversity that makes a sister.*" They will stick with you and rejoice when you rejoice and to hold up in prayer when trials come; they will encourage and correct, in love. They will be there, no matter what.

God will use them in your life, for His glory, for your good, and forever. Pat and I, the sisters who never knew a stranger, we also love to people watch as a pastime. Sometimes we get to know people on retreats as the Lord leads them in our path. These are "God encounters," and we enjoy them so. Sometimes these are my favorite parts of the retreat. I know God has brought us together for that purpose. In almost every retreat that I can remember, Pat has spotted four elderly ladies eating out; they looked *very old* to us at first when we were in our twenties. Now I must admit, these days, they don't look quite so very old as they once did!

Pat will always pop up with joy, put a bubbly smile on her face, and say, "That is going to be us when we get to be that age." We all us laugh in agreement. I smile secretly thinking and questioning God, *Are we all really going to be* that *old one day?*

As I finish this book God has called me to write, I think to myself, *Pat was right, that* is *going to be us when we get old, sitting down eating lunch together.*

Then I realize with a groan that God's Spirit anointed Pat to say that all along because that is us. We "4 for the Mountaintop" retreat sisters have stood the test of time; it was a "God thing" all along. He held us together over thirty-plus years with His spirit and with His love! We are growing old together but not too old together. We applaud God; it is His will; may He be glorified. God always gives me what to write; today He gave me the last word for this chapter; it fits. "We must know that we have

...it to be a number in the world, not just to go for ...hat work. We have been created to love and to ...Teresa inspires us to pray:

...in my life so that I can do your will in this glory. In Jesus name use Anne, Pat, Debbie and

...what God can do with one weakened vessel and what He ...ty vessels. Seek His face. Do you want more of Jesus? Pray with ...your heart. See what God will do with you. Our journeys are all ...you ask God to send you faith, the journey will lead you to live in the center of His heart to be held in the palm of His hand. Enjoy the ride and don't forget to treasure the people you meet along the way. It makes it all worth it, the glorious risen Jesus. May God be glorified in all you do!

If you have any questions or comments, call or email me. Thanks for listening! If this book has blessed you, pass it on. Share the Good News!

CHAPTER 17

The Last Word
The Alpha and the Omega

This group of four has been retreating together for almost over thirty years. That's commitment, my friend. We have laughed together, cried together, been pregnant together, nursed our babies together, shared our lives, shared our wisdom, shared our hearts, and, most importantly, shared our prayers together. Retreats are planned and enjoyed by all, and our hearts are filled with precious memories.

We delight in sharing with all we meet, on retreat weekend, that altogether, we have twenty-two children. People just roll their eyes at us. In our younger days, our dear sister Pat used to point out a group of old and gray senior women in a foursome, like us, and say, "That's us in twenty years." Well, I guess you could say she was prophetic, and the joke's on us—as now, over thirty years later, we are those women, older and grayer and wiser for the journey. I trust these ladies with my life. We have learned to trust each other's correction, as well as each other's encouragement, and tremendous growth has happened because of our commitment to retreat together. This is my recipe for women to be able to grow spiritually: retreat two times a year with three other trusted friends. You'll be glad you did.

Now we are all nanas (grandmas). Grandparents are a gift from God. I personally feel that one of the grandparent's roles is to pass on their faith to their grandchildren. So that's just what I try to do whenever I am with one of my fourteen grandchildren. My one grandchild Bella had what we called "Nana and me" days. When Bella was four, I often sang songs to Jesus and talked about our God. One spring day, we even

preschool bulletin board and acted out the
that she wanted to do it again and again.
ained until one spring day, when Bella and
ny friend that Jesus loves her and He loves me

ɔ her best friend of the same age, I was inquisitive
took out ӕse would be. "Bella," I said with a smile in my voice,
birth oſana," she said, "she didn't know that.'" It was a moment
Yet ưs I said, "Bella, you are an evangelist because you tell people
I ɔoth burst into song with a verse of "Jesus Loves Me." I couldn't
ɔ word *me* with the words *Bella* and *Emily*, which brought uncon-
ɔ both of us. I guess Bella has been listening to Nana after all.
emplated that moment, I couldn't help but think how many adults are
ɔar-old Emily but just don't know that. Jesus loves you, and so do I. Oh,
how the body of Christ needs more evangelists like Bella to tell them this I know. Yes,
as the Bible says, "*The harvest is plentiful, but the laborers are few*" (Luke 10:2). Will
you tell someone who doesn't know that Jesus loves them like Bella did? You too can
be an evangelist, no matter what your age. You are never too old and you are never too
young to tell someone the Good News. Bella is living proof of that.

We have done the journey, "4 for the Mountaintop." Today I am in full time ministry! I am a Titus II woman who helps women find joy in their vocation as wives and
mothers. As a "mommy mentor," I lead them from the valleys of despair to the mountain of joy. I teach them how to apply the word of God to their daily life. I instruct
them in our one holy Catholic faith and encourage them to frequent the sacraments.
I lead them to the heart of God. If I had not gone to the "4 for the Mountaintop"
retreats with my favorite three sisters in Christ, my best friends, I would not have the
maturity to speak the wisdom to share that only God can give. The journey takes you
to your ministry, and you have the blisters to prove it.

I would like to publically thank Debbie, Pat, and Anne for accompanying on
the "4 for the Mountaintop" retreats. They have led me, each in their own way, to
a deeper walk with our Lord Jesus Christ. Like the disciples, we have been called to
set apart time each year to be alone with God—like Peter, James, and John at the
transfiguration.

The journey has helped me grow. The journey has made me whole. When we look back on our journey to the mountain, which spans over thirty years, we all agree—it is nothing short of miraculous.

If you do not remember anything else, ladies, please remember this pearl of great price: "Miracles Happen! The greatest miracles happen in the heart, where only God can see!" Prayerfully read this book, *4 for the Mountaintop*. Read it twice, once for content and once for discernment. Ask the Lord if He is calling you to begin a "4 for the Mountaintop" retreat. What is God calling you to do? Who is calling you to invite to the mountain? Do not be afraid. The Spirit of God will not lead you where the grace of God cannot keep you.

So dust off your Bible, get on your hiking boots, pack your bags, and book your beach retreat. Most importantly, do not forget to invite Jesus to be your guide. Remember to enjoy the view and write in your journals along the way. Nothing is impossible with God. Your "4 for the Mountaintop" journey will be your journey. Let Jesus map out a trip custom designed to bring you and your three best friends to the heart of God. Know that we will be praying for you.

This book, *4 for the Mountaintop*, was wrought in prayer and journeyed over a twenty-year span. It was lived out with three sisters and a holy living God. Now is your chance to be an evangelist by passing on the Good News to whomever God puts on your heart. Begin the journey to the mountaintop with the three Christian sisters whom God selects for you. Don't forget Jesus, your Retreat Master. Pass this book on to another that God puts on your heart.

I'm so excited about what God is going to do on your journey to the heart of Jesus on the mountain. Please write, call, or e-mail me; I'm all ears. I have a big heart for sisterhood as well.

I'd love to meet you and speak at your church. If it's on God's calendar, then it is on mine. I hold you dear sister before His throne of grace in prayer. Meet me there. Pray for me as I pray for you. *May God be glorified in all you do!*

PART 3

Your Journey: The Eight Climbs

INTRODUCTION

The question is, "Are you ready to begin a '4 for the Mountaintop' group of your own?" Let me tell you this; it will be a journey! The Webster dictionary defines a *journey* as "something suggesting travel or passage from one place to another." This is the good news because the journey you take with God and your three best friends is the most important part. It will be unlike anyone else's journey. Along the way, God will transform you from friends to *sisters in Christ* and cement your lives together in a way you could never have thought of or imagined.

That said, read the following poem and contemplate it.

Safari On!

Life is like a safari; don't you think so too?
A journey to experience, custom-made for you.
A trained guide is needed to lead the way.
A guide who diligently directs where to go, and what to say.
Watch out for the snake creeping or the gator in the waterbed.
Don't worry; a guide's eyes are trained to avoid the danger ahead.
Don't be surprised if a lion greets you with his scary "ROAR!"
I assure you, a safari, it is never a bore.
You may spot a leopard or hopping kangaroo,
Or even hear a hungry hippo growling at you.
Along with your guide, nature in all its' beauty you see.
The guide points out a rainbow or a bird perched in a tree.
It is easy to spot the zebra with stripes boldly displayed,
Careful, the rhino's coming at you as the guide shouts, "Get out of the way!"

An elephant is way too big to find a hiding place.
The graceful giraffe seems to be running a race.
While on a safari, each animal becomes a priceless view.
Pause as your guide carefully points each one out to you.
It is wise to choose a guide as you safari on in life too.
To help you avoid the pitfalls and point out the beautiful view.
Remember how varied the animals encountered on a safari day
It is the same with the people that you meet along life's way.
The roaring lions shout, desiring to be heard.
Stop a moment, and you will hear their every word.
With eyes wisely focused and ears attuned to the guide;
It becomes evident the beauty of each person on the inside.
Just like a present wrapped tightly with a pretty bow,
Take the time to both open up and listen; then, each person gets to know.
If you meet a zebra or rhino, greet with a, "How do you do!"
Don't say to them, "Why can't you just be a kangaroo?"
Ditching the lions because their roar is too loud,
Or the zebra whose stripes are way too bold,
It is really not okay,
Because you may need their gifts someday?
You may still want to avoid the snakes along the way,
But smile kindly first, then bid them, "Good day!"
Each person is created for a purpose to do,
That is why they are they, and you are you.
Be yourself, as gentle and as free as a bird,
Or be loud and bold, as a lion begging to be heard,
Be as graceful as a gazelle for heaven's sake,
Or be as growly as a gator in the lake.
If we are as patient, kind, and understanding as we can be,
We can all live together in harmony.
On life's safari tread really, really slow,
There are a lot of people to get to know.
Life is like a safari, it is true.

It's a journey to experience, custom-made for you.
So, Safari on, my friend, and do not miss the view!
On a safari day, there is always something good in store for you.

What do you think? Do you have any questions? Not to worry, I have answers, or I will find someone who does. Anne, Debbie, Pat, and I are all so different; so between the four of us, I am confident that the answer will come. We, "4 for the Mountaintop" sisters, pray about everything. Jesus always has the answer.

Common questions:

1. How do I begin?
2. Who do I invite to join me?
3. How do I explain a "4 for the Mountaintop" retreat to my friends?

In the chapters that follow, I will attempt to answer all your questions. I have divided this second part of the book into eight climbs. These climbs will walk you step by step toward having a "4 for the Mountaintop" group of your own.

Are you ready? Get your hiking boots on because it is time to climb!

THE FIRST CLIMB: DO YOU KNOW JESUS?

My hat is off to you, miss mountain climber. You have decided to take the first step of starting a "4 for the Mountaintop" retreat. You will do great. We will be praying for you. I am available to answer questions at any time. You can find my contact information at the end of the book.

Let me ask you a question. Do you know Jesus Christ? Have you accepted Him as your personal Savior? Do you want to invite Jesus to be Lord of your life?

"It is necessary to awaken again in believers a full relationship with Christ, mankind's only Savior. Only from a personal relationship with Jesus can an effective evangelization develop" (St. John Paul II).

Set your heart on Him alone. I can assure you He will lead you home. Where is home? Home is where the heart is. The journey of the heart is a work of God. You may not be able to see it yet, but one day you will. Be assured that He is working in the silence of your heart where only He resides. One day, He will unveil it to you. Wait for it, look for it! Will it cost you anything? Oh, it will cost you everything! It cost Jesus everything! It cost Mary everything! It cost Job, John the Baptist, Peter, and Paul. It cost Mother Teresa, Pope John Paul II, and all the saints before us everything: all their time, talent, and treasure. What did they receive in return? There is no comparison to the great graces God will bestow on those who love Him. This world has nothing worthwhile to offer those who walk the way of the cross with a Holy God. On the journey, you learn God alone suffices. But oh, it is worth the road trip because it is a climb toward the heart of God. The journey ends when you are face to face with our Savior in our heavenly home.

As you know from reading part I, I met Jesus at seven years old at my first communion. He spoke to my heart as I received the Body of Christ that day. The gift of faith was poured into my soul. I was a Catholic schoolgirl whose heart was set on God alone. The teachings given by the nuns had laid a great foundation. Their daily example in word and deed caused my heart to cry out, "All I want is to know Jesus Christ and the power of His rising." My grandmother, Amata Morono, a faithful and true servant of Christ, nourished it with her love and through her example.

What if you had not been given a firm foundation of your Catholic faith? The following are ways to get to know Jesus:

1. Seek the Lord in daily prayer.
2. Frequent the sacraments.
3. Join a Bible study at your church.
4. Go and talk to a priest or deacon.
5. Sign up for RCIA.
6. Watch Catholic TV and listen to Catholic radio (e.g., EWTN).
7. Read the lives of the saints.
8. Choose Catholic friends.
9. Go to a Catholic prayer group.
10. Read the daily readings for Mass.

Before you can start a "4 for the Mountaintop" retreat, you need to know the retreat master, Jesus Christ. Anyone can take a trip to the beach or the mountains with their three best friends, but if you desire it to be a retreat, Jesus needs to be invited to come along. I encourage you to get to know Jesus for yourself, and He will guide you to an unforgettable "4 for the Mountaintop" retreat. He will build the relationships of the four of you into a sisterhood that will last a lifetime.

Remember the day of your conversion and journal your testimony, or give your testimony to someone. Our life in Christ can be passive and dull, or we can be filled with the Holy Spirit and live a life fully alive in Christ. You have a choice.

Jesus invites you to walk in His footsteps. Are you willing to die to *self* and surrender all each day? Walking with Christ comes at a cost. It is a free gift that will cost you everything! To follow Christ requires a death of self. Do not be afraid of His ways because He loves you and will guide you with His Fatherly love.

Scriptures

Read the following scriptures, contemplate them, and then write down your thoughts.

1. *To know Him (Christ Jesus my Lord) and the power of his resurrection and [the] sharing of his sufferings by being conformed to his death.* (Philippians 3:10)

   _____

   _____

   _____

   _____

   _____

2. *Ask and it will be given to you; seek and you will find; knock and the door will be opened to you.* (Mathew 7:7)

   _____

   _____

   _____

   _____

   _____

3. *On that journey as I drew near to Damascus, about noon a great light from the sky suddenly shone around me. I fell to the ground and heard a voice saying to me, "Saul, Saul, why are you persecuting me?" I replied, "Who are you, sir?" And He said to me, "I am Jesus the Nazorean whom you are persecuting."* (Acts 26:13–15)

   _____

   _____

   _____

   _____

   _____

4. *Now this is eternal life, that they should know you, the only true God, and the one whom you sent, Jesus Christ.* (John 17:3)

_____

_____

_____

_____

_____

5. *He said to them, "But who do you say that I am?" Simon Peter said in reply, "You are the Messiah, the Son of the living God.* (Mathew 16:15–16)

_____

_____

_____

_____

_____

6. *No one has greater love than this, to lay down one's life for one's friends.* (John 15:13)

_____

_____

_____

_____

_____

7. *Martha, burdened with much serving, came to him and said, "Lord, do you not care that my sister has left me by myself to do the serving? Tell her to help me." The Lord said to her in reply, "Martha, Martha, you are anxious and worried about many things. There is need of only one thing. Mary has chosen the better part and it will not be taken from her."* (Luke 10:40–42)

_____

_____

_____

_____

8. *When Elizabeth heard Mary's greeting, the infant leaped in her womb, and Elizabeth, filled with the Holy Spirit, cried out in a loud voice and said, "Most blessed are you among women, and blessed is the fruit of your womb.* (Luke 1:41–42)

_____

_____

_____

_____

_____

Scripture Reflection

God made us to know Him, to love Him, and to serve Him. He is waiting patiently for you to seek after Him. Those who do are never the same again.

Did you ever play hide-and-seek with a preschooler? You say to them, "You hide, and I will count." Off they run to hide. You count, "One, two, three, four, five, six, seven, eight, nine, ten," and then shout, "Ready or not, here I come!" As you begin the hunt, looking to and fro, out they pop even before your eyes are upon them.

"Here I am, mommy," they say, giggling with glee. They could not wait. They were so happy to be found. If we seek Him, we will find Him. Can't you almost hear Him say, "Here I am. You found me!" He can't wait to have you find Him.

It does not matter if you find Jesus as I did at seven years old in the Eucharist or like St. Paul did when he was knocked off his horse. He was running a hundred miles an hour in the wrong direction. Paul, like most good Jews, knew the law. What did he do with his head full of the Torah? Like they say, "He threw the book at the people." Despite Paul's blindness, Jesus opened his eyes and gave him a spiritual sight to see Jesus face to face. Paul learned that Jesus came to fulfill the law by laying down His life for His people. Jesus did not abandon the law but brought the law of love.

Maybe God will have you journey along like Peter learning from Jesus daily as a disciple before He cements in your soul a conversion. Perhaps Jesus is your friend like Martha and Mary. One day, He will reveal Himself to you as Savior and Lord. It matters not how you find Jesus; the important thing is to find Him. May your heart's cry be, "All I want is to know Jesus Christ and the power of His rising?"

Our Father in heaven desires that all His children come to know Him and cultivate a relationship with Him daily and all your life. "For God so loved the world that he gave His only Son, so that everyone who believes in Him might not perish but might have eternal life" (John 3:16). Cultivate a daily prayer life and frequent the sacraments. Who knows, your "4 for the Mountaintop" sisters may be attending the same Mass, waiting for you to meet them. Pray and seek the face of God.

Questions

1. Who is Jesus to you? A Friend? A Brother? Your Savior? Your Lord? Do you know Him, not just about Him?

   _____

   _____

   _____

   _____

   _____

2. Did you ever get knocked off your horse like St. Paul? In what areas of the faith were you "blind?" How did Jesus change you through it?

   _____

   _____

   _____

   _____

   _____

3. Is Jesus calling you to a deeper walk with Him? God wants us all in. Are you? Read the book of Acts. How can you put more in common?

   _____

   _____

   _____

   _____

   _____

4. Peter's eyes were opened so that he saw Jesus for who He really was. Peter cried out, "You are the Christ, the Son of the living God." How did this transformation take place?

_____
_____
_____
_____
_____

5. Have you ever felt that you lost Jesus? What did you do?

_____
_____
_____
_____
_____

6. What does surrendering cost? What did it cost Mary, Peter, and Paul?

_____
_____
_____
_____
_____

7. Are you ready to give your heart to Jesus today? What is holding you back?

_____
_____
_____
_____
_____

Let us pray:

Dear Heavenly Father,

All I want is to know You. I want to walk with You like Peter and Paul. I want to be Your friend as Martha and Mary were. I want to surrender my life to You like the Blessed Mother. Jesus, please come into my heart and be my Savior. I give my life to You. Fill me with Your love. Open my eyes so I can see. I ask this in Jesus's name, amen!

The Challenge:

Commit to going to confession as soon as possible and maybe monthly. Attend daily Mass often. Have a daily prayer time and read the scriptures of the day. Journal each day what God is doing in your life.

Questions, concerns, ideas?

_____

_____

_____

_____

_____

Wow—you have made it through the first climb!

THE SECOND CLIMB: TO LOVE GOD

Do you love God? What is love to you? In Scripture, we discover what the word love means according to God:

> *If I speak in human and angelic tongues but do not have love, I am a resounding gong or a clashing cymbal. And if I have the gift of prophecy and comprehend all mysteries and all knowledge; if I have all faith so as to move mountains but do not have love, I am nothing. If I give away everything I own, and if I hand my body over so that I may boast but do not have love, I gain nothing. Love is patient, love is kind. It is not jealous, [love] is not pompous, it is not inflated, it is not rude, it does not seek its own interests, it is not quick-tempered, it does not brood over injury, it does not rejoice over wrongdoing but rejoices with the truth. It bears all things, believes all things, hopes all things, endures all things. Love never fails. If there are prophecies, they will be brought to nothing; if tongues, they will cease; if knowledge, it will be brought to nothing. For we know partially and we prophesy partially, but when the perfect comes, the partial will pass away. When I was a child, I used to talk as a child, think as a child, reason as a child; when I became a man, I put aside childish things. At present we see indistinctly, as in a mirror, but then face to face. At present I know partially; then I shall know fully, as I am fully known. So faith, hope, love remain, these three; but the greatest of these is love. (1 Corinthians 13:1–13)*

There are three kinds of love: *philos*, *eros*, and *agape*. God loves us with everlasting love. "God so loved the world that He sent His only begotten Son, that whoever believes in Him shall not perish but have everlasting life" (John 3:16). No greater love has no man than to lay down his life for his brothers.

Wow, who has that kind of love for God? Will you please stand up, only kidding! I know the answer. No one can possibly love God with an everlasting love, as He loves us. When we were but sinners, Christ died for us. No one has a love on their own that gives them the ability to lay down their life for their brothers. We depend on His amazing grace to love one another. St. Teresa says, "It is all grace."

As we get to know God, we begin to understand the kind of love He has for us, *agape*. You see, we love Him because He first loved us. Even the love we have is a gift of the Holy Spirit. He fills us with His love. We come to discover as we get to know God that it is impossible to love on our own accord. We try and fail over and over again.

We also discover that there is no magic wand. We must choose the fruits of the Holy Spirit over our flesh. It is like exercising a muscle. The more we use our muscles, the stronger we become. We use it, or we lose it.

In other words, the more we love, the more love God pours into our soul. We must empty ourselves to be filled with the Spirit and God's love. Daily and prayerfully, we surrender the flesh that brings death and sin and then ask God to fill us with more of Him. Remember the words of the old song, "I want more of Jesus, more and more and more, I want more of Jesus than I've ever had before, I want more of His great love, so rich and full and free, I want more of Jesus so I'll give Him more of me."

There comes the point in our life when we get to know ourselves. It is then that we come face to face with ourselves and see who we really are—sinners. It is then that we realize how much we need a Savior. We begin to seek Jesus and return to our faith. We discover that God is love, and our love begins to grow. Slowly but surely, we let more and more of Jesus into our hearts. Eventually, maturity takes place. Then our life becomes a thank you card for what He has done for us.

How do you get to love Jesus?

1. Surround yourself with mature Catholics who know Him.
2. Begin a daily prayer time.
3. Read Scripture and put it into practice.
4. Practice virtue.
5. Get a mentor (see Titus 2:5–?).
6. Take baby steps toward Jesus.
7. Get a spiritual director or a confessor.

8. Choose a prayer partner.
9. Frequent Mass and reconciliation.
10. Read the catechism.

You will need the fruits of the Holy Spirit to grow in your heart if your "4 for the Mountaintop" retreats are going to last a lifetime. Ask yourself this question, "Do you want to go to the mountain top with Jesus with your three best friends, or are you just looking for a girls' getaway to the beach?" If you want to go to the mountaintop with our Lord and your three best friends, it will take work. I encourage you to take the climb. I promise it will be worth the effort. The love of Christ grown in the hearts of each retreat sister is the only thing that will cement the relationships in Christ. All of you will long to go away and climb the mountain with our Lord together, year after year.

Remember you will get out of the "4 for the Mountaintop" sisterhood what you put into it! What are you willing to sacrifice out of love for Christ? Make a decision today to not only know Jesus but also to take the time to love Him, for to know Jesus Christ is to love Him. Your heart will be filled with His love, so you can truly love others.

Scriptures

Read the following scriptures, contemplate them, and then write down your thoughts.

1. *As Jesus passed on from there, He saw a man named Matthew sitting at the customs post. He said to him, "Follow me." And he got up and followed Him.* (Matthew 9:9)

   _____

   _____

   _____

   _____

   _____

2. *When they had finished breakfast, Jesus said to Simon Peter, "Simon, son of John, do you love Me more than these?" He said to Him, "Yes, Lord, You know that I love You." He said to him, "Feed my lambs." He then said to him a second time,*

"Simon, son of John, do you love Me?" He said to Him, "Yes, Lord, You know that I love You." He said to him, "Tend My sheep." He said to him the third time, "Simon, son of John, do you love Me?" Peter was distressed that he had said to Him a third time, "Do you love Me?" and he said to Him, "Lord, You know everything; You know that I love you." (Jesus) said to him, "Feed My sheep." (John 21:15–17)

_____

_____

_____

_____

_____

3. *He (Jesus) got into a boat and his disciples followed him. Suddenly a violent storm came up on the sea, so that the boat was being swamped by waves; but he was asleep. They came and woke Him, saying, "Lord, save us! We are perishing!" He said to them, "Why are you terrified, O you of little faith?" Then He got up, rebuked the winds and the sea, and there was great calm. (Matthew 8:23–26)*

_____

_____

_____

_____

_____

4. *When the disciples saw him walking on the sea they were terrified. "It is a ghost," they said, and they cried out in fear. At once (Jesus) spoke to them, "Take courage, it is I; do not be afraid." Peter said to him in reply, "Lord, if it is You, command me to come to You on the water." He said, "Come." Peter got out of the boat and began to walk on the water toward Jesus. But when he saw how (strong) the wind was he became frightened; and, beginning to sink, he cried out, "Lord, save me!" Immediately Jesus stretched out his hand and caught him, and said to him, "O you of little faith, why did you doubt?" (Matthew 14:26–31)*

_____

_____

_____

_____

_____

5. *Standing by the cross of Jesus were His mother and His mother's sister, Mary the wife of Clopas, and Mary of Magdala. When Jesus saw His mother and the disciple there whom he loved, He said to His mother, "Woman, behold, your son." Then He said to the disciple, "Behold, your mother." And from that hour the disciple took her into His home.* (John 19:25–27)

_____
_____
_____
_____
_____

6. *If I speak in human and angelic tongues but do not have love, I am a resounding gong or a clashing cymbal. And if I have the gift of prophecy and comprehend all mysteries and all knowledge; if I have all faith so as to move mountains but do not have love, I am nothing. If I give away everything I own, and if I hand my body over so that I may boast but do not have love, I gain nothing. Love is patient, love is kind. It is not jealous, (love) is not pompous, it is not inflated, it is not rude, it does not seek its own interests, it is not quick-tempered, it does not brood over injury, it does not rejoice over wrongdoing but rejoices with the truth. It bears all things, believes all things, hopes all things, endures all things. Love never fails. If there are prophecies, they will be brought to nothing; if tongues, they will cease; if knowledge, it will be brought to nothing. For we know partially and we prophesy partially, but when the perfect comes, the partial will pass away. When I was a child, I used to talk as a child, think as a child, reason as a child; when I became a man, I put aside childish things. At present we see indistinctly, as in a mirror, but then face to face. At present I know partially; then I shall know fully, as I am fully known. So faith, hope, love remain, these three; **but the greatest of these is love.*** (1 Corinthians 13)

_____
_____
_____
_____
_____

7. *No one has greater love than this, to lay down one's life for one's friends.* (John 15:13)

_____

_____

_____

_____

_____

8. *Lord, You have probed me, You know me: You know when I sit and stand; You understand my thoughts from afar. You sift through my travels and my rest; with all my ways You are familiar. Even before a word is on my tongue, Lord, You know it all. Behind and before You encircle me and rest Your hand upon me. Such knowledge is too wonderful for me, far too lofty for me to reach. Where can I go from Your spirit? From Your presence, where can I flee? If I ascend to the heavens, You are there; if I lie down in Sheol, there You are. If I take the wings of dawn and dwell beyond the sea, Even there Your hand guides me, Your right hand holds me fast. If I say, "Surely darkness shall hide me, and night shall be my light"— Darkness is not dark for You, and night shines as the day. Darkness and light are but one. You formed my inmost being; You knit me in my mother's womb. I praise You, because I am wonderfully made; wonderful are Your works! My very self You know. My bones are not hidden from You, When I was being made in secret, fashioned in the depths of the earth. Your eyes saw me unformed; in Your book all are written down; my days were shaped, before one came to be.* (Psalm 139:1–16)

_____

_____

_____

_____

_____

Scripture Reflection

The Bible is the living word, sharper than a two-edged sword. As you read the Bible, it is reading you. Reread the above scriptures slowly and out loud and concentrate on how much God loves you. Each time you take time alone to pray, ask Jesus to speak to you through His Word. Most importantly, put into practice what you read. Pray, wait, listen, and do!

God loves you. This is a fact. Jesus died, just for you; this is a *truth*. You must spend the time with Jesus to let this truth sink deep into your soul. Peter could never have walked on water if he did not know Jesus and how much Jesus loved him. The disciple could never have stood at the foot of the cross as Jesus took His last breath if he had not had a great love for Him. Peter, James, and John would not have gone to the mountaintop with Jesus unless He had loved and taught them. They put their trust in God alone.

This week, learn to love God and let His love fill your soul.

Questions

1. In the book of Mathew, God calls some to be His disciple. They put down their nets and come at once. Has God called you to be His disciple? What do you need to lay down to be His disciple? Search your heart in prayer.

     _____

     _____

     _____

     _____

     _____

2. Why did Jesus ask Peter three times, "Do you love Me?" If Jesus asked you, "Do you love Me?" What would be your response?

     _____

     _____

     _____

     _____

     _____

3. Jesus was asleep on the boat when the storm came. They woke Him up, and He calmed the storm. Who do you call when the storms arise in your life? Where do you go?

     _____

     _____

     _____

     _____

     _____

4. Why was Peter able to walk on water? There were so many disciples in the boat, but why was Peter the only one to climb out of the boat? Would you have climbed out of the boat? Would you have walked on water?

_____

_____

_____

_____

_____

5. One disciple was at the foot of the cross as Jesus took His last breath? Where did all Jesus' friends go? Would you have stood there with Jesus? Why do you think Jesus chose that disciple to take care of the blessed Mary, His mother?

_____

_____

_____

_____

_____

6. Read one line of 1 Corinthians 13 verses 4 to 8 and practice that virtue. Keep practicing until your heart grows in that virtue. How did you do?

_____

_____

_____

_____

_____

7. No greater love has a one than to lay down your life for your friends. Who have you laid down your life for? Who has done that for you?

_____

_____

_____

_____

_____

8. You are fearfully and wonderfully made. What is God asking you to do? Is He asking you to start a "4 for the Mountaintop" retreat group of your own? Is He asking you to begin the climb?

_____

_____

_____

_____

_____

You have almost finished the second climb!

Do you want to leap over the mountain and volunteer to be the organizer? If your answer is yes, you have taken on a significant role in the process. You have taken on the challenge to be the organizer of your group, at least for now. You are also being called upon to host the first luncheon with your three best friends:

1. Spend a few weeks in prayer before you begin.
2. Quiet your soul and listen for God to direct you.
3. Journal your thoughts each day.
4. Seek the Lord about who you should invite to be your companions to the mountaintop.
5. In the adoration chapel, ask God if you should organize "4 for the Mountaintop" retreats.
6. Pray about each woman you want to invite.
7. Journal what you feel God speaking to you.
8. Patiently wait on God.

Let us pray:

Dear Heavenly Father,

I want to know You more each day and fall in love with You. I want to follow You and be taught by You like Your disciples were. Please teach me Your ways and fill me with Your love. Jesus, meek and humble of heart, make my heart like unto You. Oh, Sacred Heart of Jesus, have mercy on me, a sinner!

The Challenge:

Commit this week to fifteen minutes of prayer and Scripture reading each day. Journal your thoughts. At the end of the day, quiet your soul and reflect on your day. Then confess your sins to Jesus. Say an act of contrition:

> *My God, I am sorry for my sins with all my heart. In choosing to do wrong and failing to do good, I have sinned against You whom I should love above all things. I firmly intend, with Your help, to do penance, to sin no more, and to avoid whatever leads me to sin. Our Savior Jesus Christ suffered and died for us. In His name, my God, have mercy.*

Questions, concerns, ideas?

_____

_____

_____

_____

_____

Wow, you have completed the second climb! Thank God for His amazing grace!

THE THIRD CLIMB: TO SERVE GOD

To anyone who has ever climbed a mountain, it may start easy, and then the climb gets progressively more challenging as time goes by. So before this climb begins, I need to ask you a question. Did you take the time last week to go to the adoration chapel? Did you ask Him if He has called you to begin a "4 for the Mountaintop" retreat? What was His answer? If it was a yes, then God may be calling you to host the first luncheon.

I always say, "No one can do everything, but everyone can do something to build the kingdom of God." God has a plan for you. He wants to use you in your gifts to build the kingdom of God. God's plan will bring you great joy, and you will be blessed for it. That is why I put the eight climbs at the end of the book. I hope you are enjoying the eight steps. My son Tyler suggested adding them to the book, and it indeed was God-inspired!

Everyone knows if you want to serve the Lord, you must let Him lead you, guide you, and call you on. We are all on a learning curve. We can't teach what we do not know. The journey takes you to your ministry. If this is your ministry, then I applaud God for you. It is a journey that you will never forget.

Again, I will be there for you every step of the way. Every climb you take, I am a phone call or an email away. I will speak at your church, zoom into your group, or bring some sisters in Christ to share about our mountaintop retreats. So let us begin the third climb!

Now is the time to put on your hiking boots and do not look back. Are you thirsty? You will need to drink a lot of water on this climb, living water, that is. Only water from the Word of God will quench your soul.

Jesus says, "But whoever drinks the water I shall give will never thirst; the water I shall give will become in him a spring of water welling up to eternal life" (John 4:14).

The Word of God, the sacraments, and the fellowship with the brethren are all lifelines and lead us to Jesus our Lord. Let Jesus teach you each day from His Word. One of the best ways to do that is to read the Word of God until it a portion pops out at you. Then pause and ask Jesus three questions:

1. What is it saying?
2. What is it saying to me?
3. How can I apply it to my life?

There is no right or wrong answer. God will speak to your heart in a way you can understand Him. So be still and know that He is God. God will change us within as we spend time with Him. This is how we get to know God's voice. "In quietness and confidence shall be our strength."

To know God is to love God; to love God is to serve God. We must take the climbs one by one. If we do not know God, how can we love Him? If we only know about Him, we might become rule-bound. Knowing Him helps us grow to love Him and serve out of that love rather than duty or pride. Take the climb! Let Jesus guide you to the mountaintop and show you the view. Let Him teach you His ways and ask Him how He wants you to serve Him. Finally, it will be time to lead others up to the mountain to seek His face. So here are ways to serve Jesus:

1. Reread the first climb to know Jesus.
2. Reread the second climb to love Jesus
3. Write down your growth from the first two chapters and applaud God for it.
4. Write what you have not done in the chapters and work on them this week.
5. Concentrate on the scriptures in each of the chapters.
6. Ask yourself what is it saying? What is it saying to me? How can I apply it to my life?
7. After asking the questions, "Do whatever God tells you to do."
8. Call or email me and let me help if need be.
9. Continue to climb. Listen for God's still, small voice.

Scriptures

Read these scriptures, contemplate them, and then write down your thoughts.

1. *To each individual the manifestation of the Spirit is given for some benefit. To one is given through the Spirit the expression of wisdom; to another the expression of knowledge according to the same Spirit; to another faith by the same Spirit; to another gift of healing by the one Spirit; to another mighty deed; to another prophecy; to another discernment of spirits; to another variety of tongues; to another interpretation of tongues. But one and the same Spirit produces all of these, distributing them individually to each person as he wishes.* (1 Corinthians 12:7–11)

_____

_____

_____

_____

2. *For thus said the Lord GOD, the Holy One of Israel: By waiting and by calm you shall be saved, in quiet and in trust shall be your strength. But this you did not will.* (Isaiah 30:15)

_____

_____

_____

_____

3. *Mary said, "Behold, I am the handmaid of the Lord. May it be done to me according to your word." Then the angel departed from her.* (Luke 1:38)

_____

_____

_____

_____

4. *The Lord said to Abram: "Go forth from your land, your relatives, and from your father's house to a land that I will show you. I will make of you a great nation, and I will bless you; I will make your name great, so that you will be a blessing. I will bless those who bless you and curse those who curse you. All the families of the earth will find blessing in you." Abram went as the Lord directed him, and Lot went with him. Abram was seventy-five years old when he left Haran.* (Genesis 12:1–4)

_____

_____

_____

_____

_____

5. *God said to Noah: "I see that the end of all mortals has come, for the earth is full of lawlessness because of them. So I am going to destroy them with the earth. Preparation for the flood. Make yourself an ark of gopherwood, equip the ark with various compartments, and cover it inside and out with pitch..." Noah complied; he did just as God had commanded him.* (Genesis 6:13–14, 22)

_____

_____

_____

_____

_____

6. *Be still and know that I am God! I am exalted among the nations, exalted on the earth.* (Psalm 46:11)

_____

_____

_____

_____

_____

7. *If we say, "We have fellowship with Him," while we continue to walk in darkness, we lie and do not act in truth. But if we walk in the light as He is in the light, then we have fellowship with one another, and the blood of his Son Jesus cleanses us from all sin.* (1 John 1:6–7)

_____
_____
_____
_____
_____

8. *Martha, burdened with much serving, came to Him and said, "Lord, do You not care that my sister has left me by myself to do the serving? Tell her to help me." The Lord said to her in reply, "Martha, Martha, you are anxious and worried about many things. There is need of only one thing. Mary has chosen the better part and it will not be taken from her."* (Luke 10:40–42)

_____
_____
_____
_____
_____

9. *He (Jesus) said, "Go into the city to a certain man and tell him, 'The teacher says, "My appointed time draws near; in your house I shall celebrate the Passover with my disciples."'"* (Matthew 26:18)

_____
_____
_____
_____
_____

Scripture Reflection

In order to serve God, you must know God, love God, and know yourself. Pray that these scriptures teach you who you are. Each of these Bible characters teaches us about how God calls you to serve in your gifts. Your service will fit your gifts and your personality. Pray that your service will delight your soul! It is time to get to know yourself better in the next chapter.

Questions

1. Reread 1 Corinthians 12 and ask the Holy Spirit to show you your gifts!

_____
_____
_____
_____
_____

2. How do you serve the Lord with gladness? What gifts do you use in the church? In your home? In your neighborhood? What gifts make you come alive?

_____
_____
_____
_____
_____

3. Spend some time in prayer, then ask yourself, *Have I gotten to know God better?* Are you loving God more? Have you learned to quiet your soul and listen to the voice of God?

_____
_____
_____
_____
_____

4. Mary was called by God to be the mother of Jesus. What was her response? How do you respond when God calls you to a *work* for Him?

_____
_____
_____
_____
_____

5. Abraham answered God's call. What was he called to do?

_____
_____
_____
_____
_____

6. What did God call Noah to do for Him? What was his response?

_____
_____
_____
_____
_____

7. Be still and know that He is God. Ask your Heavenly Father what you can learn from Mary, Abraham, and Noah. What is He calling you to do?

_____
_____
_____
_____

8. Why do sisters need sisters? Which three sisters can you think of that lead you toward heaven? Begin to pray for them and discern if God is calling them to be a part of your "4 for the Mountaintop" group?

_____

_____

_____

_____

_____

9. Martha and Mary were sisters who each had different gifts. How are you like Mary? How are you like Martha?

_____

_____

_____

_____

_____

10. Jesus gave a feast at the last supper with his closest companions. Why the feast and what can you learn from their relationships?

_____

_____

_____

_____

_____

You have almost finished the third climb. Great job!

Let us pray:

Dear Heavenly Father,

I want to know You, love You, and serve You. First, I need to discover who I am. Let me quiet my soul and listen for Your still, small voice that teaches me who I am and who You are. I want to do Your will, like Mary, Abraham, and Noah. I am waiting for You to call me. I ask this in Jesus's name, amen!

The Challenge:

Spend time in the Scripture and ask yourself these three questions:

1. What is it saying?
1. What is it saying to me?
2. How can I apply it to my life?

Questions, concerns, ideas?

_____
_____
_____
_____
_____

Amazing! You have made it to the top of the third climb!
Are you thirsty yet?

THE FOURTH CLIMB: ACCESSORIZE WITH VIRTUE

High fives!! Double exclamation marks!! You are halfway up the mountain. This is your journey.

This is important; in order to go to the mountaintop with God and your three best friends, you need to begin to grow into the image and likeness of Christ in your personal walk with Him. Galatians 5:22–23 says it best: "In contrast, the fruit of the Spirit is love, joy, peace, patience, kindness, generosity, faithfulness, gentleness, self-control. Against such there is no law."

> As Jesus was walking by the Sea of Galilee, He saw two brothers, Simon, who is called Peter, and his brother, Andrew, casting a net into the sea; they were fishermen. He said to them, "Come after Me, and I will make you fishers of men." At once, they left their nets and followed Him. (Matthew 4:18–20)

Did you ever wonder what drew the disciples to faith in Jesus? Was it what Jesus said, or was it what Jesus did? Both what He said and did motivated them to follow Him. Most importantly, Jesus called them by name. He took a personal interest in each of them. He, like a shepherd, guided them and protected them. He trained them to be His disciples and taught them to be "fishers of men!"

The same is true today. Jesus calls us by name. He takes a personal interest in each of us. The more we obey His voice, the more He leads us, guides us, and protects us. The more we empty ourselves of sin, the more He fills us with His love and grace. If we let Him, He will also make us "fishers of men!" Following in the footsteps of

Jesus in word and in deed will draw others to Christ. In the Book of Romans, we are encouraged to "put on the Lord Jesus Christ and make no provision for the desires of the flesh" (Romans 13:14).

Being full of the Holy Spirit and choosing to walk in virtue and His grace aid you in living a joy-filled, holy, blessed life in Christ. Take an honest assessment of your life and your heart.

Let us take a look at what accessories you are storing in the jewelry box of your heart. Did you find in the box some "pearls of great price?" This necklace was purchased through obedience to Christ, bought on the road of suffering. Now you proudly display them not just on special occasions but as a daily accessory. Pearls speak volumes in saying, "I found my Jesus, and I will never let Him go." Are there bands of gold within your heart, waiting to come out of your mouth to speak a word of wisdom, exhortation, or correction? A well-trained tongue of a disciple is essential in drawing others to Jesus. If you let Jesus lead your words, you will someday be walking on the "streets of gold." Has Jesus put an invisible crown upon your head and placed jewels in it for the deeds done by you in love for Him? Will you one day place your crown at the feet of Jesus, bringing glory to His name?

As you come face to face in the mirror with yourself, you may find that some imitation jewelry has found its way into your jewelry box. Some of these accessories you possibly bought into as a young Christian and are now ready to exchange "a fake it 'til you make it" mentality for an authentic character. Maturity teaches that all flesh has to be purified in the furnace of God's love. We all know a diamond is formed by tremendous pressure, becoming a thing of beauty. Let God polish, prune, and test your character, then lead you from sin and death to life and peace.

Most people can detect genuine quality character from a put-on. We want to have hearts set on Christ alone. Let virtue and character be your accessory of choice. Be patient with yourself because virtue takes time to develop.

Growing Fruits

In contrast, the fruit of the Spirit is love, joy, peace, patience, kindness, generosity, faithfulness, gentleness, self-control. Against such, there is no law. Now those who belong to Christ (Jesus) have crucified their flesh with its passions and desires.

—Galatians 5:22–24

One day I was grocery store shopping, and I happened to be in the fruit department. I heard the Holy Spirit speak in His still, small voice, "I am going to give you the fruit of self-control." I stopped dead in my tracks. I was so overcome with the fruit of joy that I was about to jump for joy. Instead, I decided to ask a question, "How are you going to give me self-control, Lord?" It was more of a dare than a question. I knew I desperately need that fruit. The answer came before I barely got the question out. God said, "I am going to give you the fruit of the self-control just like I gave you the fruit of patience." I decided not to jump after all, or run, or leap either. Instead, I took a pause and a deep breath. Then I took a trip down memory lane with my Jesus.

I recounted the day when God began to plant the fruit of patience in my heart. It was in the seventies. I, a new mom, had a two-week-old girl named Tarolyn and an almost-two-year-old boy named Tyler. I was getting ready to buckle them in for safety when Tyler said, "Mommy, I want to buckle up myself." He spoke with an exclamation point at the end of his sentence. This became a daily choice to let Tyler buckle his seatbelt all by himself. I purposed to exercise my virtue of patience. I forced a pretend smile. Some days this was easier to do than others.

Along the way, I grew in patience as Tyler grew in independence and responsibility. At first, I found myself counting to ten under my breath as my firstborn Tyler buckled himself. As I matured, I was able to willingly wait patiently. I tried to avoid the temptation to hurry him toward success. By encouraging the growth in learning new skills, instead of correcting, or rushing, learning took place. On a good day, I would respond rightly with, "Sure, son, go ahead. You are such a big boy."

Tyler tried and tried again. Try he did until he mastered the skill. Tyler became an "I want to do it myself champion." Tyler led the way, and his six siblings followed after him, eager to learn new skills all by themselves. Each of my seven children learned to do many things: from toilet training to homework, from driving a car to living on their own. I was glad I chose to patiently let them go and fly their wings. They have soared.

God was right! As I look back on my life to the day in the fruit department, I see that I grew in self-control, just like I grew in patience. It took time, effort, and prayer.

Will you be ready to throw down your nets at the sound of His voice calling your name? He may be calling you to be His disciple. Be still in prayer and listen for His still voice then do whatever He tells you! This is how we walk in Jesus's footsteps on the journey from vice to virtue. You must travel light if you want to fly on the wings of eagles. Not too light to accessorize with virtue. Virtue will never weigh you down.

When we grow in virtue, we become more like Christ. So begin to cast down imagination and sin and let more of Jesus in. Grace and peace are given to those who have crucified themselves to Christ. Paul says, "I no longer live, but Christ lives in me."

I speak to a lot of groups on virtue and growth in Christ. The tagline for my Little Pink Dress Ministry is "Accessorize with virtue." Along with your pearl necklace and matching earrings, put on joy, love, peace, patience, kindness, goodness, faithfulness, and fear of the Lord.

Scriptures

Read the following scriptures, contemplate them, and then write down your thoughts.

1. *In contrast, the fruit of the Spirit is love, joy, peace, patience, kindness, generosity, faithfulness, gentleness, self-control. Against such there is no law. Now those who belong to Christ (Jesus) have crucified their flesh with its passions and desires.* (Galatians 5:22–24)

   _____
   _____
   _____
   _____
   _____

2. *As (Jesus) was walking by the Sea of Galilee, He saw two brothers, Simon who is called Peter, and his brother Andrew, casting a net into the sea; they were fishermen. He said to them, "Come after Me, and I will make you fishers of men." At once they left their nets and followed Him.* (Matthew 4:18–20)

   _____
   _____
   _____
   _____
   _____

3. *Go and assemble all the Jews who are in Susa; fast on my behalf, all of you, not eating or drinking night or day for three days. I and my maids will also fast in the same way. Thus prepared, I will go to the king, contrary to the law. If I perish, I perish!* (Esther 4:16)

    _____

    _____

    _____

    _____

    _____

4. *Then the angel said to her, "Do not be afraid, Mary, for you have found favor with God.* (Luke1:30)

    _____

    _____

    _____

    _____

    _____

5. *Love is patient, love is kind. It is not jealous, (love) is not pompous, it is not inflated, it is not rude, it does not seek its own interests, it is not quick-tempered, it does not brood over injury, it does not rejoice over wrongdoing but rejoices with the truth. It bears all things, believes all things, hopes all things, endures all things. Love never fails.* (1 Corinthians 13:4–8)

    _____

    _____

    _____

    _____

    _____

6. *She is clothed with strength and dignity, and laughs at the days to come. She opens her mouth in wisdom; kindly instruction is on her tongue. She watches over the affairs of her household, and does not eat the bread of idleness. Her children rise up and call her blessed; her husband, too, praises her: "Many are the women of proven worth, but you have excelled them all." Charm is deceptive and beauty fleeting; the woman who fears the Lord is to be praised.* (Proverbs 31:25–30)

_____

_____

_____

_____

_____

7. *Let us not grow tired of doing good, for in due time we shall reap our harvest, if we do not give up.* (Galatians 6:9)

_____

_____

_____

_____

_____

8. *For this very reason, make every effort to supplement your faith with virtue, virtue with knowledge, knowledge with self-control, self-control with endurance, endurance with devotion, devotion with mutual affection, mutual affection with love.* (2 Peter 1:5–7)

_____

_____

_____

_____

_____

Scripture Reflection

Virtue grows each day as you practice it. Put on Christ each day and be a reflection of His love to all you meet. We are the hands of Christ that He is fashioning for His purposes. The disciples were chosen, called, trained, and then sent out to be Jesus's disciples. Jesus is still calling people in the same way to be His disciples. He trains them up, and then He sends them out to be fishers of men. Will you answer His call? Will you drop your nets and come at once to follow Him?

Questions

1. Are you walking in the fruits of God's Spirit, or are you walking in the flesh? What is the easiest virtue for you to practice? What is the most difficult vice to overcome?

   _____

   _____

   _____

   _____

   _____

2. Is God calling you to be a fisher of men?

   _____

   _____

   _____

   _____

   _____

3. What is the secret to Esther's beauty? How did she use her beauty for God's glory?

   _____

   _____

   _____

   _____

   _____

4. Mary is full of grace. How can you model Mary and walk in His grace?

   _____

   _____

   _____

   _____

   _____

5. How can you grow in the virtue of Love? Love encompasses all of the virtues combined.

_____

_____

_____

_____

_____

6. Proverbs 31 says, "A perfect wife, who could find one?" How can you take baby steps toward becoming a Proverbs 31 woman?

_____

_____

_____

_____

_____

7. The more you practice virtue, the more virtue grows in your heart. What steps can you take toward accessorizing with virtue each day?

_____

_____

_____

_____

_____

Let us pray:

Dear Jesus,

I want to follow You wherever You lead me. I want to be Your disciple. Please train me to follow You and make me a fisher of men. I ask this in Jesus's name, amen!

The Challenge:

What vices are weighing you down? Take a retreat and discern what virtue the Spirit is calling you to grow in your life? Life gives us many choices. Choose virtue over vice; it is *God*'s choice. What we choose is what we become. Choose one of the fruits of the Spirit to concentrate on. How about choosing patience or self-control?

Questions, concerns, ideas?

_____

_____

_____

_____

_____

THE FIFTH CLIMB: CHOOSING YOUR COMPANIONS

Give yourself a high five, a pat on the back, and maybe a jump for joy! Now applaud God. He alone takes a bow. Oh, what the Lord can do with one yielded vessel!

"You've come a long way, baby!" It is still uphill all the way, but oh, the joy set before you! You are flying on the wings of eagles with Jesus as the wind beneath your *wings*. If you have made it this far, God is most likely leading you to start a "4 for the Mountaintop" retreat group.

You are not walking this journey alone. It is a journey of faith. You need God's help to make it to the top of the mountain. He will lead you as you ascend the mountain. You may not see Him, hear Him, or feel Him, however, by faith, you know that He is guiding you. Trust me; He will never leave you nor forsake you.

Soon God will call three faithful companions to accompany you. Who will He choose? You can choose your own friends, but it would be better if you let Jesus select them. A good friend would be a ton of fun to go away with for a girl's getaway. However, a godly friend would be a better choice for a yearly retreat. Without God's help, you might end up just taking a beach trip instead of a "4 for the Mountaintop" retreat.

Let God choose! Only God knows whose heart is set on Him. Only God knows who is willing and able to put on those hiking boots and climb up the mountain. Only God sees inside the hearts. God is all knowing. I encourage you to leave the choice up to God.

How do you let God choose? You wait, and you pray. Begin today to center your life on Christ. Begin to put what you have learned on the climbs thus far into practice. Just as Jesus called His disciples Peter, James, and John, and He will call forth your "4 for the Mountaintop" retreat sisters. Your journey will not be like anyone else's journey to the mountain, and neither will theirs. Pray for Jesus to give your eyes to see and ears to hear. Pray for your heart to be set on Him alone.

As God begins to show you the three retreat sisters, one by one, pray for confirmation. Then invite them to lunch, first, one sister at a time, then all three sisters. This may seem like a long span of time, but it will bear much fruit in the long run. In my walk with Christ, I have found that patience gains all things. "They that hope in the Lord will renew their strength, they will soar on eagles' wings; They will run and not grow weary, walk and not grow faint" (Isaiah 40:31).

God gives His best to those who leave the choice up to Him. Look at how God chose David, the shaped boy. What means did God use to replace Judas? Remember again how God chose His disciples. God knows which people would be the best choices for your retreat sisters. So let Him join you together. These will be godly women who you can trust with your heart. These will be women with who you can be yourself. If you are crying buckets of tears, these women will have Kleenex already available in their pockets. If you stumble and fall, these women will catch you. These women will have your back. These women will walk in step with Jesus alongside you. These women will forever be your "4 for the Mountaintop" sisters because God will cement you together with His love.

If you have already chosen the three friends to go to the retreats with, continue to meet with them for lunch monthly. Get to know each other, grow to love one another as sisters, and begin to serve one another. Each time you get together, pray with one another. Begin to discern if the four of you are compatible with taking a retreat together. Wait and pray and give God the time needed to knit your lives together. God's timing is everything; wait until God calls you to go to the mountaintop. Until then, enjoy getting to know one another. Most of all, get to know God.

It is time to thank God for what He is doing in your midst. He is calling you to go to the mountaintop soon and very soon. Get ready, ladies, for the best is yet to come!

Scriptures

Read the following scriptures, contemplate them, and then write down your thoughts.

1. *But if any of you lacks wisdom, he should ask God who gives to all generously and ungrudgingly, and he will be given it. But he should ask in faith, not doubting, for the one who doubts is like a wave of the sea that is driven and tossed about by the wind.* (James 1:5–6)

   _____
   _____
   _____
   _____
   _____

2. *You need endurance to do the will of God and receive what he has promised. "For, after just a brief moment, he who is to come shall come; he shall not delay."* (Hebrews 10:36–37)

   _____
   _____
   _____
   _____
   _____

3. *They that hope in the Lord will renew their strength, they will soar on eagles' wings; They will run and not grow weary, walk and not grow faint.* (Isaiah 40:31)

   _____
   _____
   _____
   _____
   _____

4. *Who can find a woman of worth? Far beyond jewels is her value. Her husband trusts her judgment; he does not lack income. She brings him profit, not loss, all the days of her life. She seeks out wool and flax and weaves with skillful hands. Like a*

merchant fleet, she secures her provisions from afar. She rises while it is still night, and distributes food to her household, a portion to her maidservants. She picks out a field and acquires it; from her earnings she plants a vineyard. She girds herself with strength; she exerts her arms with vigor. She enjoys the profit from her dealings; her lamp is never extinguished at night. She puts her hands to the distaff, and her fingers ply the spindle. She reaches out her hands to the poor, and extends her arms to the needy. She is not concerned for her household when it snows—all her charges are doubly clothed. She makes her own coverlets; fine linen and purple are her clothing. Her husband is prominent at the city gates as he sits with the elders of the land. She makes garments and sells them, and stocks the merchants with belts. She is clothed with strength and dignity, and laughs at the days to come. She opens her mouth in wisdom; kindly instruction is on her tongue. She watches over the affairs of her household, and does not eat the bread of idleness. Her children rise up and call her blessed; her husband, too, praises her: "Many are the women of proven worth, but you have excelled them all." Charm is deceptive and beauty fleeting; the woman who fears the Lord is to be praised. Acclaim her for the work of her hands, and let her deeds praise her at the city gates. (Proverbs 31:10–31)

_____

_____

_____

_____

_____

5. *Then Jesus came with them to a place called Gethsemane, and he said to his disciples, "Sit here while I go over there and pray." He took along Peter and the two sons of Zebedee, and began to feel sorrow and distress. Then he said to them, "My soul is sorrowful even to death. Remain here and keep watch with me."* (Matthew 26:36–38)

_____

_____

_____

_____

_____

6. *Standing by the cross of Jesus were His mother and His mother's sister, Mary the wife of Clopas, and Mary of Magdala. When Jesus saw His mother and the disciple there whom He loved, He said to His mother, "Woman, behold, your son." Then He said to the disciple, "Behold, your mother." And from that hour the disciple took her into His home.* (John 19:25–27)

_____
_____
_____
_____
_____

7. *A friend is a friend at all times, and a brother is born for the time of adversity.* (Proverbs 17:17)

_____
_____
_____
_____
_____

8. *Blessed are the poor in spirit, for theirs is the kingdom of heaven. Blessed are they who mourn, for they will be comforted. Blessed are the meek, for they will inherit the land. Blessed are they who hunger and thirst for righteousness, for they will be satisfied. Blessed are the merciful, for they will be shown mercy. Blessed are the clean of heart, for they will see God. Blessed are the peacemakers, for they will be called children of God. Blessed are they who are persecuted for the sake of righteousness, for theirs is the kingdom of heaven. Blessed are you when they insult you and persecute you and utter every kind of evil against you [falsely] because of me. Rejoice and be glad, for your reward will be great in heaven. Thus they persecuted the prophets who were before you.* (Matthew 5:3–12)

_____
_____
_____
_____
_____

9. *While they were eating, He took bread, said the blessing, broke it, and gave it to them, and said, "Take it; this is My body." Then He took a cup, gave thanks, and gave it to them, and they all drank from it. He said to them, "This is My blood of the covenant, which will be shed for many. Amen, I say to you, I shall not drink again the fruit of the vine until the day when I drink it new in the kingdom of God." Then, after singing a hymn, they went out to the Mount of Olives.* (Mark 14:22–26)

_____

_____

_____

_____

_____

10. *Do not be led astray: "Bad company corrupts good morals." Become sober as you ought and stop sinning. For some have no knowledge of God; I say this to your shame.* (1 Corinthians 15:33–34)

_____

_____

_____

_____

Scripture Reflection

Jesus handpicked His disciples. In the same way, He will choose your "4 for the Mountaintop" sisters. As He called them by name, each disciple came at once. Do you hear His voice? How will you respond?

Yes, first Jesus called them. Then Jesus taught them. He cemented them as a band of brothers with His love. Lastly, He breathed on them the Holy Spirit. Then He sent them out to teach others. They all had their mission to fulfill. What is He calling you to do?

Questions

1. The book of James tells us if we want wisdom, we must ask in faith and believe. Ask Jesus for wisdom and write down what He is telling you to do.

    _____
    _____
    _____
    _____
    _____

2. Patience gains all things. Are you waiting on God, or are you giant's steps ahead of His calling for you? Wait, pray, and then journal whatever He tells you.

    _____
    _____
    _____
    _____
    _____

3. Do you want to wait upon the Lord and fly on the wings of eagles, or do you want to do it your way?

    _____
    _____
    _____
    _____
    _____

4. Jonathan loved David more than himself. Do you have a friendship where sisters love you in such a godly way? How can you build a sisterhood like David and Jonathon's friendship?

    _____
    _____
    _____
    _____

4 FOR THE MOUNTAINTOP RETREATS

5. Jesus chose only Peter, James, and John to accompany Him on three occasions: healing of Jairus's daughter, transfiguration, and praying in the Garden of Gethsemane. Why might He have done this?

    _____

    _____

    _____

    _____

    _____

6. Jesus called twelve men to be His disciples. How many were at the foot of the cross to say goodbye? Why? Do you see why John was the disciple He loved?

    _____

    _____

    _____

    _____

    _____

7. Have you ever made a friend who becomes a sister because she stood with you through adversity?

    _____

    _____

    _____

    _____

    _____

8. How long did Jesus teach His disciples? What did He teach them? Have you let Jesus teach you?

    _____

    _____

    _____

    _____

    _____

9. What pops out at you at the Last Supper?

_____
_____
_____
_____
_____

10. Choose your friends wisely? What are your criteria for choosing a friend? What are God's criteria?

_____
_____
_____
_____
_____

Let us pray:

Dear Heavenly Father,

Please choose my "4 for the Mountaintop" retreat sister. I know You will do a better job than I could ever do. You see the heart, Lord Jesus, of all. Please choose the sisters whose hearts are set on You. Cement us with Your love. Let us become sisters in Christ. I surrender all to You. I ask this in Jesus's name, amen!

The Challenge:

Take time in prayer to choose the three sisters to accompany you on your journey but leaving the choice up to God. I encourage you to wait on Him. It will be worth the wait.

Questions, concerns, ideas?

_____
_____
_____
_____

Congratulations! You have made it through the fifth climb. Grab a tambourine and do the victory dance. Thank the Lord Jesus for what was, what is, and what is to come. It is going to be an exciting climb because now you have godly gals to accompany you. Before you is a faith-filled adventure. Never forget to let Jesus be your guide. He knows the way up the mountain. Polish up your hiking boots, ladies.

THE SIXTH CLIMB: GETTING TO KNOW ONE ANOTHER

Hoorah! It is the sixth climb! You have climbed a long way up! You are almost to the top of the mountain. I can't wait until you see the view from the top.

This chapter is one of the most important chapters in the book. Please read it carefully and prayerfully. The friends that you bring to the mountain top with you will determine if you are going to be retreat sisters for life or just your one and only retreat together.

You must each ask yourself, *Do I want a deeper walk with the Lord Jesus or just go on a getaway girls' weekend*? Each of the women must seek the Lord in prayer and discover what God is telling her. Be still, quiet your soul, and let God speak to you. You must be honest with yourself and with God. Friends are awesome, but when you are choosing retreat sisters, it is important that their hearts are set on God. Each must also be on board with the other women in the group. Unity is key to a retreat to the mountains. Not to worry, it takes time to discern, so take it slow. It also takes a journey.

After you discern God's choice of sisters, begin by hosting a simple luncheon with just the four of you. If you keep it simple, you will be able to easily host it monthly. The host is like a facilitator. She is key in starting a group and is responsible for keeping the group going. She needs to be able to lead and to follow well, be organized, diplomatic, kindhearted, patient, and persistent. She should know upfront that she will have to give more than she receives. God will bestow upon her many blessing for stepping into these shoes. If you are not gifted with some of these virtues, pray that God will call one of the other three women to be the facilitator.

Our "4 for the Mountaintop" group began by just getting together for lunch at my home. We tried to get together at my home monthly. Sometimes we chose to meet at a restaurant. I must say that meeting at someone's home is always cozier. The home enables your group to talk freely, bring nursing babies to, and kick back and enjoy each other. Getting to know one another for women comes naturally. Have a lead-in question ready. Be sure and ask each woman to share a little about themselves. Opening up may take time.

A word to the wise keeps the conversation on a godly plane. Have a no-gripping zone established in advance. Remind the women to let no gossip pass through their lips. If the conversation does turn toward gossip, nip it in the bud. Pray for God to help you to encourage and correct one another in love. When you get together, let 1 Corinthians 14:26 be your guide: "So, what is to be done, brothers? When you assemble, one has a psalm, another an instruction, a revelation, a tongue, or an interpretation. Everything should be done for building up." Girl talk comes easy to most. Have questions ready on hand, just in case. The purpose of the luncheon is to get to know one another.

Here are some ice breaker questions:

1. Tell the story of how you met your husband.
2. Tell us a little about your family.
3. Would you like to share your testimony?
4. What is your favorite Scripture?

This luncheon should open the door to getting together a second time. When eating and sharing around the table, the conversation should flow smoothly. Praying together joins your hearts and helps you to focus on Jesus. During your chat time, explain to them what you are trying to do. Show them the book and encourage them to buy a copy. Better yet, if you feel like being generous, purchase a copy for each of the women in your group and send it home with them as a souvenir. Ask them to read the first part of the book. Remember to end the luncheon by interceding for each other. Ask everyone to bring their calendars. Before the women head home, be sure and pencil in a second luncheon.

If peace was the fruit of the luncheon, then you have picked a great group of women. Hopefully, these will be your "4 for the Mountaintop" retreat sisters. Watch for any red flags, though, and make a mental note. Then discuss these issues at the second luncheon. Early on, problems may arise, and handling them quickly is a wise choice. Women are complicated. Think about this; it might have just been a bad day for someone. Be careful not to kick anyone off the island yet. Give them a second chance. However, if a red flag continues, take it to prayer and discern. Even when you are journey along on God's perfect will for you, you may meet a giant or two. You may have to walk through the desert or hear a lion roar. Keep your eyes on Jesus. Don't be surprised if He teaches you to walk on water. Never give up. Effort plus prayer equals victory in Jesus. Keep on doing what is right, and in due time, you will reap a harvest.

Now let us see what God's Word has to say.

Scriptures

Read the following scriptures, contemplate them, and then write down your thoughts.

1. *Jonathan and David made a covenant, because Jonathan loved him as his very self.* (1 Samuel 18:3)

    _____

    _____

    _____

    _____

    _____

2. *She had a sister named Mary [who] sat beside the Lord at his feet listening to him speak. Martha, burdened with much serving, came to him and said, "Lord, do You not care that my sister has left me by myself to do the serving? Tell her to help me." The Lord said to her in reply, "Martha, Martha, you are anxious and worried about many things. There is need of only one thing. Mary has chosen the better part and it will not be taken from her."* (Luke 10:39–42)

    _____

    _____

    _____

    _____

    _____

3. *After some time, Paul said to Barnabas, "Come, let us make a return visit to see how the brothers are getting on in all the cities where we proclaimed the word of the Lord." Barnabas wanted to take with them also John, who was called Mark,*

but Paul insisted that they should not take with them someone who had deserted them at Pamphylia and who had not continued with them in their work. So sharp was their disagreement that they separated. Barnabas took Mark and sailed to Cyprus. (Acts 15:36–39)

_____

_____

_____

_____

_____

4. *Finally, brothers, whatever is true, whatever is honorable, whatever is just, whatever is pure, whatever is lovely, whatever is gracious, if there is any excellence and if there is anything worthy of praise, think about these things.* (Philippians 4:8)

_____

_____

_____

_____

_____

5. *There are friends who bring ruin, but there are true friends more loyal than a brother.* (Proverbs 18:24)

_____

_____

_____

_____

_____

6. *The Lord God has given me a well-trained tongue, that I might know how to answer the weary, a word that will waken them. Morning after morning he wakens my ear to hear as disciples do.* (Isaiah 50:4)

_____

_____

_____

_____

_____

7. *All who believed were together and had all things in common; they would sell their property and possessions and divide them among all according to each one's need. Every day they devoted themselves to meeting together in the temple area and to breaking bread in their homes. They ate their meals with exultation and sincerity of heart, praising God and enjoying favor with all the people. And every day the Lord added to their number those who were being saved.* (Acts 2:44–47)

_____

_____

_____

_____

_____

8. *One of His disciples, the one whom Jesus loved, was reclining at Jesus' side.* (John 13:23)

_____

_____

_____

_____

_____

Scripture Reflection

Life is complicated. Sometimes a shoe fits just fine until you wear it. It is the same way with friendships. I learned at an early age to let God choose my friends. He knows everything about them and me. He knows what each of us needs to follow Him. A retreat sister is a person that scripture speaks about when it says, "A friend is a friend at all times, but it is adversity that makes a brother."

Both Paul and Peter were called to be God's disciples, yet they could not get along with each other. Paul instead chose Barnabas, the encourager, to be his companion, while Peter chose John to be his. Most of us cannot get along with everyone. Let God do the choosing, and He will provide the grace needed to climb the mountain together. He will also bring the grace needed to build relationships.

Questions

1. How did Jonathon prove his love to David? How did David and Jonathan grow their relationship?

   _____

   _____

   _____

   _____

   _____

2. Mary and Martha are sisters, yet they are very different. How did that help them to build a relationship? How did that hinder their relationship?

   _____

   _____

   _____

   _____

   _____

3. Give examples of why one should live out the Philippians 4:8 scripture. Share about a time you have been hurt by someone not living that scripture? Share about how you have hurt someone with your *tongue*.

   _____

   _____

   _____

   _____

   _____

4. Tell the story of a true friendship that you've had in Christ? What was the fruit?

   _____

   _____

   _____

   _____

   _____

5. Has God given you a well-trained tongue of a disciple? What is God saying to you through this scripture?

_____

_____

_____

_____

_____

6. God builds His people into communities. Are you a part of a church community?

_____

_____

_____

_____

_____

7. Why might one of the disciples be beloved? How can you be more like him?

_____

_____

_____

_____

_____

Let us pray:

Dear Heavenly Father,

Thank you for calling us to be the "4 for Mountaintop Sisters." This is a special relationship and responsibility. May we always keep you in the center of our hearts, our sisterhood, our lives, and our retreats. We thank you in advance for the work of God that we are embarking on. Give us the grace to climb the mountain together in unity. I ask this in Jesus' name, amen!

The Challenge:

Do something special for each sister in your group this week. Send a card, give a call, make a meal, or say a prayer for each sister. A relationship is built by doing little things with great love.

Questions, concerns, ideas?

_____

_____

_____

_____

_____

The sixth climb is super-duper complete! Jumping for joy or applauding God once again, let the relationships begin. I see a "4 for the Mountaintop" retreat ahead. Buckle your seat belts. It will be the ride you've been waiting for. Get ready to pack your bags. Did someone say, "Girls' getaway?" No, it is retreat time! Can't you see a "4 for the Mountaintop" retreat growing right before your eyes? "For the vision is a witness for the appointed time, a testimony to the end; it will not disappoint. If it delays, wait for it, it will surely come, it will not be late" (Habakkuk 2:3).

SEVENTH CLIMB: WE'RE ON OUR WAY

Dear "4 for the Mountaintop" sisters,

Do you remember the day you began the climb toward your very own "4 for the Mountaintop" retreats? I want to encourage you with the words of St. Teresa of Ávila, "God withholds nothing from those who persevere." Keep on moving forward because this will be a work of God that He is designing just for the four of you. As I said before, no two retreats are alike. You are each fearfully and wonderfully made. God will custom-make the retreats ahead in such a way to fit perfectly for each of you. That is if you continue to ask Him to come along and be your retreat master. Nothing is impossible with God. I can do all things through Christ who strengthens me.

Your journey began weeks or even months ago but has only really just started. Keep on praying and keep on seeking. The words to an old children's song, "I Am a Promise," come to mind. Here is the chorus:

> *If you're listening, you will hear God's voice.*
> *If you are trying, He will help you make the right choice,*
> *Because you are a promise you see,*
> *A great big bundle of potentiality.*

Let the God of the universe design the blueprint. God, the architect of your souls and journeys, now joins them together for your retreat.

When you are confronted with any problems to solve or need to make a decision, take it to prayer. Encourage each sister to seek the Lord. Then come together and share what God is saying to you. Do not move forward until you are all in agreement, and all are peaceful. Remember, peace is your barometer.

You can purchase a journal to document your "4 for the Mountaintop" journey. Learn to quiet your soul in prayer, listen, and then do whatever God tells you. "Trust in the Lord with all your heart, on your own intelligence do not rely; In all your ways be mindful of Him, and He will make straight your paths" (Proverbs 3:5–6).

Your first "4 For the Mountaintop" retreat will be the most memorable. It will be like having your first child. You are walking into the unknown and learning as you go journey.

Will you make mistakes? Of course, you will!

Will you offend each other? I'd like to say no, but with humility established in my conscience, I must admit you probably will. Will there be a lot of laughter? Yes, there will. I must add that you will shed a few tears too.

We are women who were created with tender hearts full of love. We love big, and we feel things big. That's us. A word to the wise, someone bring the Kleenex. Take lots of pictures and make a "4 for the Mountaintop" scrapbook.

I am not going to describe how to go on the first "4 for the Mountaintop" retreat. Here's why:

1. There is a guideline in the first part of the book.
2. Let God guide you through His Holy Spirit.
3. I am praying for you to have the retreat that fits you best.
4. I am an email away. Ask me anything. If I do not have the answer, someone will.
5. Let prayer and scripture be your GPS.
6. May your retreat be the adventure of a lifetime!
7. Do not forget to invite Jesus to be your retreat master.
8. Begin each retreat with a special prayer. You can write your own prayer or use a prayer like the prayer of St. Francis or the rosary.

The prayer of St. Francis

Lord, make me an instrument of your peace, Where there is hatred, let me sow love; where there is injury, pardon; where there is doubt, faith; where there is despair, hope; where there is darkness, light; where there is sadness, joy;

O Divine Master, grant that I may not so much seek to be consoled as to console; to be understood as to understand; to be loved as to love.
For it is in giving that we receive; it is in pardoning that we are pardoned; and it is in dying that we are born to eternal life.

Scriptures

Read the following scriptures or words of the Saints, contemplate them, and then write down your thoughts.

1. St. Teresa of Ávila said, "God withholds Himself from no one who perseveres." What are Your thoughts on this? Don't you just want to praise Him?

    _____
    _____
    _____
    _____
    _____

2. St. Bernard said, "Everything begins in prayer, everything ends in prayer."

    _____
    _____
    _____
    _____
    _____

3. *Then the Lord said: Go out and stand on the mountain before the Lord; the Lord will pass by. There was a strong and violent wind rending the mountains and crushing rocks before the Lord—but the Lord was not in the wind; after the wind, an earthquake—but the Lord was not in the earthquake; after the earthquake, fire—but the Lord was not in the fire; after the fire, a light silent sound.* (1 Kings 19:11–12)

    _____
    _____
    _____
    _____
    _____

4. *Here in the wilderness the whole Israelite community grumbled against Moses and Aaron... The Israelites ate the manna for forty years, until they came to settled land; they ate the manna until they came to the borders of Canaan... After they made the journey from Rephidim and entered the wilderness of Sinai, they then pitched camp in the wilderness. While Israel was encamped there in front of the mountain, Moses went up to the mountain of God. Then the Lord called to him from the mountain, saying: This is what you will say to the house of Jacob; tell the Israelites: You have seen how I treated the Egyptians and how I bore you up on eagles' wings and brought you to myself. Now, if you obey me completely and keep my covenant, you will be my treasured possession among all peoples, though all the earth is mine. You will be to me a kingdom of priests, a holy nation. That is what you must tell the Israelites. (Exodus 16:2, 35, 19:2–5)*

_____

_____

_____

_____

_____

5. *The word of the Lord came to Jonah, son of Amittai: "Set out for the great city of Nineveh, and preach against it; for their wickedness has come before me." But Jonah made ready to flee to Tarshish, away from the Lord... The Lord, however, hurled a great wind upon the sea, and the storm was so great that the ship was about to break up... Then they picked up Jonah and hurled him into the sea, and the sea stopped raging... But the Lord sent a great fish to swallow Jonah, and he remained in the belly of the fish three days and three nights... Then the Lord commanded the fish to vomit Jonah upon dry land... So Jonah set out for Nineveh, in accord with the word of the Lord. Now Nineveh was an awesomely great city; it took three days to walk through it. (Jonah 1:1–4, 15; 2:1, 11; 3:2–3)*

_____

_____

_____

_____

_____

6. *God said to Noah: "I see that the end of all mortals has come, for the earth is full of lawlessness because of them. So I am going to destroy them with the earth. Preparation for the Flood. Make yourself an ark of gopherwood, equip the ark with various compartments, and cover it inside and out with pitch..." For forty days and forty nights heavy rain poured down on the earth. On the very same day, Noah and his sons Shem, Ham, and Japheth, and Noah's wife, and the three wives of Noah's sons had entered the ark, together with every kind of wild animal, every kind of tame animal, every kind of crawling thing that crawls on the earth, and every kind of bird... And when the waters had swelled on the earth for one hundred and fifty days... Gradually the waters receded from the earth. At the end of one hundred and fifty days, the waters had so diminished that, in the seventh month, on the seventeenth day of the month, the ark came to rest on the mountains of Ararat. (Genesis 6:13–14; 7:12–14, 24; 8:3–4)*

_____

_____

_____

_____

_____

7. *When they had departed, behold, the angel of the Lord appeared to Joseph in a dream and said, "Rise, take the child and his mother, flee to Egypt, and stay there until I tell you. Herod is going to search for the child to destroy him." Joseph rose and took the child and his mother by night and departed for Egypt. He stayed there until the death of Herod, that what the Lord had said through the prophet might be fulfilled, "Out of Egypt I called my son." (Matthew 2:13–15)*

_____

_____

_____

_____

_____

8. *After six days Jesus took Peter, James, and John his brother, and led them up a high mountain by themselves. And He was transfigured before them; His face shone like the sun and His clothes became white as light.* (Matthew 17:1–2)

Scripture Reflection

We are all on a journey with God. It begins in prayer. Then God asks you to give a surrender, yes. He guides you each step of the way. He leads you on an unknown path. He teaches you along the journey to know Him, to love Him, and to serve Him.

God called Moses to lead His people to the Promised Land. God called Jonah to speak to the people of Nineveh. He called Noah to build an ark and sail to safety with an ark full of animals and his family. God called Mary to be the mother of His Son, Jesus. God called Peter, James, and John to go away with Him. God called the saints to point the way to Jesus.

It took trust, obedience, and perseverance to follow the plan God had put before them. What seemed impossible at first became a reality. They, like Job, could say, "I heard about You from my friends, but 'now I know You for myself.'" The journey is what leads you to the heart of God. To know Him is to love Him, and to love Him is to serve Him and one day be happy with Him in heaven.

To each one of us He calls, He provides grace, wisdom, and a GPS to follow. It is God working through His Spirit. He uses people who have gone the path before us, scripture, the saints, the sacraments, and the Holy Spirit. Pause a minute and thank God for what He has done for you. Repent from any mistrust, disobedience, or complaining you have done along the journey. Do you need to ask anyone's forgiveness? If yes, pray and go repair the relationship!

Questions

1. God always answers prayer. He says, "Yes, no, or wait." Give an example of a time you persevered in prayer as you waited on God to answer your prayer.

    _____
    _____
    _____
    _____
    _____

2. What are your thoughts on the quote of St. Bernard? How can you parallel it to the forming of your "4 for the Mountaintop" retreat?

    _____
    _____
    _____
    _____
    _____

3. Elijah wanted to hear God's voice. Did he hear it in the cave? In the wind? Where did he hear God's voice? How do you best hear God's voice? Share a time God spoke to you, and you knew it was His voice.

    _____
    _____
    _____
    _____
    _____

4. God called Moses to take a journey through the Red Sea. Picture yourself in the group Moses was leading. Were you afraid? Did you cry out for quail? Did you want to turn back?

    _____
    _____
    _____
    _____
    _____

5. Jonah took a journey with God. Pretend you are Noah, and God calls you to speak to the people of Nineveh. Would you do it? Or do you find yourself in the belly of a whale?

   _____
   _____
   _____
   _____
   _____

6. Noah took a journey with God. If you were Noah, would you build the ark according to the specifications or do it your way? What would life be aboard that ark: noisy, smelly, cramped? Did you realize that God Himself closed the door of the ark?

   _____
   _____
   _____
   _____
   _____

7. Mary took a journey with God. "May it be done unto me according to Thy word." Mary gave her surrendered "yes." Have you given yours? What did it cost Mary? What has it cost you?

   _____
   _____
   _____
   _____
   _____

8. Peter, James, and John took a journey with Jesus. Where did they go? How is their journey with God to the mountains similar to yours? Did you notice the words, "All they could see was Jesus?" Who do you see?

   _____
   _____
   _____
   _____
   _____

Let us pray:

Heavenly Father,

You have been so good to me. Thank You for calling me to journey with You and my "4 for the Mountaintop" sisters. We have been on an adventure I will never forget. Being alone with You gave me a new skip in my step, refreshed my soul, and drew us all closer to gather. Like the disciples before us, I wanted to build three booths and stay forever. Now help me to continue the journey with an obedient heart full of thanksgiving. I cannot wait to return. I ask this in Jesus's name, amen!

The Challenge:

Work to keep up the relationships that God is weaving together. Plan monthly luncheons. Pray for each other.

Questions, concerns, ideas?

_____
_____
_____
_____
_____

When God begins a journey with you and your retreat sisters, He will finish it. Thank Him that He withholds nothing from those who persevere. Keep on moving forward. Keep on doing what is right, and in due time, you will reap a harvest. Harvest time is coming.

EIGHTH CLIMB: FACING THE GIANTS

My friend Debbie one time taught me a life lesson many years ago. I was complaining to her about not having time to write. What was her wise advice? She said, "I have found that if something is important enough to me, I will make the time to do it." This word has passed the test of time. It has served me well, and now I pass it on to you as a souvenir from this book.

What is important to you? Money? Fame? Friends? Or a relationship with Jesus? Hopefully, as we near the top of the mountain and the finish line of this book, you have discovered that there are friends, and then there are friends who become closer than sisters in Christ. My friend Karen, who was my mentor for a short time, often says, "Choose the friends that lead you heavenward."

The reason for the eight climbs on the journey is to guide you to have a fruitful retreat experience. The "4 for the Mountaintop" sisters will be a souvenir that you want to treasure all the days of your life. These will be sisters that you want to nurture, encourage, and even correct in love. One of my favorite quotes that I coined is, "I care, and I will be there." I coined that phrase because I mentor women, but only the number of women that I can take care of. I am not about numbers; I am about being there for those I have committed to being there for. In some seasons, when my husband or children or parents need me, I cannot take on any women at all. Sometimes I can take one or two. In other seasons, I can take on five to seven. It all depends on the season that I am in. "There is an appointed time for everything, and a time for every affair under the heavens" (Ecclesiastes 3:1).

For me, family comes first. If we put order into our lives, things fall into place: God, husband, children, parents, grandchildren, church, friends, activities, and then me. This is the order I live by. We don't want to save the whole world and lose our family. Take care of those people in your family first. God put them in your life. Trust that God will do the rest. To me, order brings peace.

That said, God made people to have relationships. However, relationships will fail or fall apart if you do not put time and effort into them. No relationships will last if they are not cared for. You must decide what is important to you. Then put your time into caring for those relationships that you want to last.

The words to a little song came to me that is a blueprint for protecting relationships:

One must water, one must weed, one must sow the precious seed. We will all work in unity to tend the garden of love.

The "4 for the Mountaintop" retreat sisters, just like your family members, need care. How do you spell care, T-I-M-E? If you water your relationships with love, weed out sin and sow the Word of God in one another's lives. You will grow a garden of unity.

As you look back on your journey, you will see that just like the mustard seed in the scriptures, you began as a small seed. Then with God's help, you grew and grew with each climb. Soon you will be strong enough to lead others to have a "4 for the Mountaintop" retreat of their own.

I am so proud of you for taking the climbs with me. Mountain climbers are bold and strong, and they persevere as commanded by God. *"I command you: be strong and steadfast! Do not fear nor be dismayed, for the Lord, your God, is with you wherever you go"* (Joshua 1:9).

Mountain climbers are embarking on new territory, not looking back but pressing forward. Does anyone remember what Caleb said to Joshua when they entered the Promised Land? Boldly and unafraid, Caleb faced the giants in the land. Does anyone remember what David, the shepherd boy, said when he faced Goliath the giant and his only weapon was a sling? Boldly and unafraid in faith, David faced the giant in the land. "David continued: 'The same Lord who delivered me from the claws of the lion and the bear will deliver me from the hand of this Philistine.' Saul answered David, 'Go! the Lord will be with you'" (1 Samuel 17:37).

Any time you relate to people, you will have relationship problems. I so want to tell you everything will be smooth sailing and calm waters ahead, but that would be a big fat lie. "I have told you this so that you might have peace in Me. In the world you will have trouble, but take courage, I have conquered the world" (John 16:33).

I can assure you that your group will encounter tests, trials, and possible *relationship* problems. This is a fact. It is not so important that problems arise but rather how you handle them when they do! Will you run away? Will you pretend that they never happened? Will you gossip to other friends and tell all? Will you face the problem head-on with boldness, deference, and love? By using God's Word as your guide, the answer to most problems that arise can be found.

Are you strong enough to face the giants?

Problem: What if one gal moves to another state?

1. Do you replace her?
2. Do you call a monthly Zoom meeting?
3. Disperse the group?

Face the giants, ladies!

Problem: What if two sisters are having trouble with each other?

1. Do you take *sides*?
2. Do you replace one or two of them?
3. Do you quit the group altogether?

Face the giants, ladies!

Problem: What if you have been in a group for ten years or so and the anointing seems gone?

1. What do you do?
2. Quit the group?
3. Find new friends?
4. Avoid meeting?

Face the giants, ladies!

Problem: What if someone wants to join your group after many years of "4 for the Mountaintop" retreats?

1. Do you not call her back or avoid her?
2. Do you try it out with five?

Face the giants, ladies!

Problem: What if a sister in your group has a personal problem? Death of a baby? Moving away and homesick? Taking care of elderly parents? Lack of funds to retreat? Marital issues?

Face the giants, ladies!

"I care, and I'll be there" should be your motto. Never have your retreat sisters needed you more than when they face a mountain in their personal life. Bring your hiking boots and help them climb. A friend is a friend at all times, but it is adversity that makes a brother or sister. Remember how many times they have been there for you and begin the climb even if you have to carry them on your back. A true friend never deserts you when you need them most.

When problems arise in your group, know that God already has the answer. Seek Him in prayer and in His Word. "Then do whatever He tells you to do." This is how you face the giants, ladies!

Scriptures

Read the following scriptures, contemplate them, and then write down your thoughts.

1. *Do not be yoked with those who are different, with unbelievers. For what partnership do righteousness and lawlessness have? Or what fellowship does light have with darkness?* (2 Corinthians 6:14)

   _____

   _____

   _____

   _____

   _____

2. *And He spoke to them at length in parables, saying: "A sower went out to sow. And as he sowed, some seed fell on the path, and birds came and ate it up. Some fell on rocky ground, where it had little soil. It sprang up at once because the soil was*

not deep, and when the sun rose it was scorched, and it withered for lack of roots. Some seed fell among thorns, and the thorns grew up and choked it. But some seed fell on rich soil, and produced fruit, a hundred or sixty or thirtyfold. Whoever has ears ought to hear." (Matthew 13:3–9)

_____

_____

_____

_____

_____

3. *He proposed another parable to them. "The kingdom of heaven is like a mustard seed that a person took and sowed in a field. It is the smallest of all the seeds, yet when full-grown it is the largest of plants. It becomes a large bush, and the 'birds of the sky come and dwell in its branches.'"* (Matthew 13:31–32)

_____

_____

_____

_____

_____

4. *How good and how pleasant it is, when brothers dwell together as one!* (Psalm 133:1)

_____

_____

_____

_____

_____

5. *Now, as He promised, the Lord has preserved me these forty-five years since the Lord spoke thus to Moses while Israel journeyed in the wilderness; and now I am eighty-five years old, but I am still as strong today as I was the day Moses sent me forth, with no less vigor whether it be for war or for any other tasks. Now give me this mountain region which the Lord promised me that day, as you yourself*

heard. True, the Anakim (giants) are there, with large fortified cities, but if the Lord is with me I shall be able to dispossess them, as the Lord promised. (Joshua 14:10–12)

6. *David answered him: "You come against me with sword and spear and scimitar, but I come against you in the name of the Lord of hosts, the God of the armies of Israel whom you have insulted. Today the Lord shall deliver you into my hand; I will strike you down and cut off your head. This very day I will feed your dead body and the dead bodies of the Philistine army to the birds of the air and the beasts of the field; thus the whole land shall learn that Israel has a God."* (1 Samuel 17:45–46)

7. *But she was greatly troubled at what was said and pondered what sort of greeting this might be. Then the angel said to her, "Do not be afraid, Mary, for you have found favor with God. Behold, you will conceive in your womb and bear a son, and you shall name him Jesus. He will be great and will be called Son of the Most High, and the Lord God will give him the throne of David his father, and he will rule over the house of Jacob forever, and of his kingdom there will be no end." But Mary said to the angel, "How can this be, since I have no relations with a man?"* (Luke 1:29–34)

8. *Then Jesus was led by the Spirit into the desert to be tempted by the devil. He fasted for forty days and forty nights, and afterwards he was hungry. The tempter approached and said to him, "If You are the Son of God, command that these stones become loaves of bread." He said in reply, "It is written: 'One does not live by bread alone, but by every word that comes forth from the mouth of God.'" Then the devil took Him to the holy city, and made Him stand on the parapet of the temple, and said to Him, "If You are the Son of God, throw Yourself down. For it is written: He will command his angels concerning you' and 'with their hands they will support you, lest you dash your foot against a stone.'" Jesus answered him, "Again it is written, 'You shall not put the Lord, your God, to the test.'" Then the devil took Him up to a very high mountain, and showed Him all the kingdoms of the world in their magnificence, and he said to Him, "All these I shall give to you, if you will prostrate yourself and worship me." At this, Jesus said to him, "Get away, Satan! It is written: 'The Lord, your God, shall you worship and Him alone shall you serve.'" Then the devil left Him and, behold, angels came and ministered to Him.* (Matthew 4:1–11)

_____

_____

_____

_____

_____

Scripture Reflection

Facing the giants doesn't frighten me! I have the Gospel as my weapon, and I am fighting on my knees.

There may be a giant or two along your journey to the top of the mountain. Not to worry, God is bigger! Fight the good fight of faith. Put on the whole armor of God.

Finally, draw your strength from the Lord and from His mighty power. Put on the armor of God so that you may be able to stand firm against the tactics of the devil. For our struggle is not with flesh and blood but with the principalities, with the powers, with the world rulers of this present darkness, with the evil spirits in the heavens. Therefore, put on the armor of God, that you may be able to resist on the evil day and, having done everything, to hold your ground. So, stand fast with your loins

ELLEN MONGAN

girded in truth, clothed with righteousness as a breastplate, and your feet shod in readiness for the gospel of peace. In all circumstances, hold faith as a shield, to quench all [the] flaming arrows of the evil one. And take the helmet of salvation and the sword of the Spirit, which is the word of God. (Ephesians 6:10–17)

You will have to fight a giant or two. Be not afraid!

God desires families and friends to work in unity. You will grow a garden of love and be a witness to all. You will look back on your mustard seed now a tree and say to yourself, "I once was a mustard seed." The "4 for the Mountaintop" sisters will see that God grew their seeds of love, faith, and perseverance into a tree strong and sturdy. Together, you will one day be a shelter to point others to Jesus.

Remember to learn from the scriptures. Be fervent in prayer. Err toward love. Never ever give up! God is growing miracles with each of your hearts. He changes us within as we spend time with Him.

Questions

1. Choose your friends wisely. Share about a time when you chose a friend that was not leading you heavenward. What was the fruit? What is the fruit with the sisters in your retreat group?

   _____

   _____

   _____

   _____

   _____

2. Sometimes we are the fertile ground, sometimes the rocky ground, and sometimes we grow weeds. What kind of ground are you on your faith walk? What kind of ground is your "4 for the Mountaintop" retreat group growing on?

   _____

   _____

   _____

   _____

   _____

180

3. Did you ever think that your mustard seed of faith would grow? What giants did you face along the way? How is the seedling doing with your retreat sisters? Have you fought a giant or two?

    _____
    _____
    _____
    _____
    _____

4. If there are giants in the land of your group, how will you fight them? What God brought peace and unity into relationships in the past where giants tried to inhabit?

    _____
    _____
    _____
    _____
    _____

5. When Caleb fought the giants, he was bold, strong, and confident in the Lord. What can you learn from the prophet Joshua? How can you use this wisdom in your group?

    _____
    _____
    _____
    _____
    _____

6. David fought a giant who was bigger and stronger and had a sword and a shield. What can you learn from David? How can you apply it to your retreat group?

    _____
    _____
    _____
    _____
    _____

7. Mary, Jesus's mother, fought many a giant. What can you learn from our blessed mother? How can you apply what you learned to your retreat group?

_____

_____

_____

_____

_____

8. Jesus is the giant slayer. His temptation in the desert shows that we do not fight against flesh and blood, but how did He overcome Satan? What lesson did you learn from Jesus and His temptations?

_____

_____

_____

_____

_____

Let us pray.

Dear Heavenly Father,

It is pleasant when brethren dwell in unity. Sometimes our flesh, the devil, or circumstances get in the way of our relationships. When that happens, help me to be bold like Joshua and strong like David, and know that you are always with me as with Mary. Help me not to give up or put my head in the sand or run away. You are knitting us together and doing a miracle in our hearts. When things get tough, help me to turn to You in prayer. You are bigger than any problem I face. You can overcome any circumstance I find myself in. May You bless my sisters and help us all learn to love one another by turning to You, waiting on You, and then doing whatever You tell us to do. I ask this in Jesus's name, amen!

The Challenge:

Pause and look at what God has done for you. Please send me a note about how your climb to the mountaintop is going. Send me a picture of your "4 for the Mountaintop" retreat sisters. Then get out your thank you cards and thank each of your retreat sisters for taking the journey to the mountain with you. Don't forget to send Jesus the biggest thank you of all!

Questions, concerns, ideas?

_____

_____

_____

_____

_____

THE VIEW AT THE TOP

My friends say that I am always talking about the journey. Most people want to arrive. Just like our children riding along on a long trip anxiously await the destination while asking, "Are we there yet? Are we there yet?" over and over again until you want them just to be still. We, the followers of Christ, seem to be asking our Heavenly Father the same question. "Are we there yet? Are we there yet?" He may be calling us to be still and know that He is God.

So few have learned to pause, look out the window, and enjoy the view. You see, we will never really arrive until we get to heaven. Along your journey, there are lessons to learn daily, weekly, monthly, and yearly. Life is a learning lesson. Day after day, God is building virtue within you. He is establishing a fortress of faith, teaching us to have our home in Him, and helping us learn the language of love. The journey is strengthening us to one day be able to teach others what we have learned. God first trains us up, and then He sends us out. The journey sometimes will take you to your ministry. The journey with Jesus takes you to the heart of God.

If you have taken the eight steps up the mountain along with your retreat sisters, you may think you have arrived. No, in reality, you have only just begun. Your journey together will continue to bring you closer to God and closer to each other. It will be the adventure of a lifetime. No two trips will look alike.

So journey on my "4 for the Mountaintop" sisters. Keep on moving forward. Keep on building your sisterhood. Keep on growing closer to Jesus. Keep on doing what is right, and, in due time, you will reap a harvest.

Each time you get the chance to go on a retreat, please take a pause and enjoy the view. What a view it will be from the top of the mountain. The memories you make and the experiences you will have together will be sewn in your heart for all eternity. Don't forget to take pictures.

If you forget all else, remember this: Ask Jesus to be your retreat master, the architect of your group, and invite Him to sit at the head of your luncheon table. Don't leave home without Him.

Remember, I am only an email away. Do not hesitate to contact me at www.ellenmongan.com and wowellen@yahoo.com.

May God be glorified in all you do! Amen! Alleluia! Glory!

The end or just the beginning!

The final bow goes to our Lord Jesus Christ!

GOD'S ARMY

We've walked the walk.
We've fought the fight.
And although we don't do everything right,
we know you, Jesus, in whom we've believed to be true
and left all behind to follow you.
We are troubled on all sides yet not distressed.
We do not despair when we're perplexed.
Persecuted but not forsaken,
cast down but not overtaken—
we trust in you with all our heart.
Your ways, O Lord, we'll not depart.
We regret nothing as we run the race to win,
casting down imaginations and every sin.
We fight the good fight of faith with our armor on,
knowing the victory you've already won.
We anxiously await your arrival in the sky,
knowing then to this world we'll say bye-bye.

It was a great blessing to share my story with you. Now please share yours with me!
Amen, alleluia, glory!

God calls us all to take the time to rest in Him, a time to draw aside and refresh at the mountain of our God. Do you hear the voice of the bridegroom calling you to just be with Him? Come!

On this mountain, Yahweh will prepare for all peoples a banquet of rich food, a banquet of fine wines, of food rich and juicy, of fine choice wines. On this mountain He will remove the mourning veil covering all peoples and shroud enwrapping all nations, He will destroy death forever. The Lord will wipe away the tears from every cheek. He will take away His people's shame everywhere on earth for Yahweh has said so. That day it will be said, see, this is our God in whom we hoped for salvation; Yahweh is the one in whom we hoped. We exult and we rejoice. That He has saved us; for the hand of Yahweh rests on this mountain.

—Isaiah 25:6–10

Come to the Mountain and Have a Peek

To Be!

To be with Thee,
oh, let it be!
Not wandering aimlessly to and fro.
To know what to do, and where to go.
To be directed by Thy Almighty hand
to follow always Your Heavenly plan
to be attuned to Your presence every step of the way,
to live a guided by God day.
To surrender my will, my time, my desires too,
oh, to surrender all, just to be with You.
To be filled with your Holy Spirit and love you,
oh, that is what I want to do!

To be one who knows the Savior's voice,
guided by Your grace to make the right choice.
To be still and know You as I pause in prayer.
To be assured that you always are there.
To follow in Your way and never be the same—
Jesus, that is the reason you came.

To walk as a disciple like Peter, John, and Paul,
to cling to the mystery of the Cross when I fall.
To be a soldier in God's army, standing strong,
leaving behind the ways of the world, not just going along.
To be a witness guiding others to You,
oh, that is what I want to do!

To take Your hand as you lead me before His Father's throne,
to be lost in His Heavenly presence; knowing I'm never alone.
To put my trust in Him; I surrender all,
thankful to have answered His call.
Oh, that is what I want to do!

So I invite you this day—
take time to pause and pray,
pour out your heart to Him each day
because Jesus is the truth, the life, and the only way.
He will lead you to the Father's throne.
You too will know that you are never alone.
Your Abba Daddy is faithful and true.
He waits patiently for you.
Oh, that is what I want to do!

To look forward to being with Him for all eternity,
praising Him with saints and angels will be quite a symphony.
To be fully alive, lost in His presence of love.
To be filled with His Holy Spirit of love.
To walk in His ways,
to sing His praise,
to know His voice,
to make the right choice,
to be still and know.
He is there wherever you go
to answer His call,
to tell one and all,

to never be alone,
to know you have a heavenly home,
oh, that just is what I want to do!

To be walking in His amazing grace,
to one day behold His holy face.
To be with Thee, my Father, my God,
just to be with You,
oh, that is just what I want to do!
To be with Thee,
my Lord, my God, oh, let it be.

GO TELL IT ON THE MOUNTAIN

While shepherds kept their watching
over silent flocks by night,
behold throughout the heavens,
there shone a holy light:
"Go, tell it on the Mountain,
"over the hills and everywhere,
"go, tell it on the Mountain,
"that Jesus Christ is born."

The shepherds feared and trembled,
when lo, above the earth
rang out the angel chorus
that hailed our Savior's birth:
"Go, tell it on the mountain,
"over the hills and everywhere,
"go, tell it on the mountain
that Jesus Christ is born!"

Down in a lowly manger
our humble Christ was born,
and God sent us salvation
that blessed Christmas morn:

"Go, tell it on the mountain,
"over the hills and everywhere,
"go, tell it on the mountain
"that Jesus Christ is born."

When I am a seeker,
I seek both night and day;
I seek the Lord to help me,
and He shows me the way:
"Go, tell it on the mountain,
"over the hills and everywhere;
"go, tell it on the mountain
"that Jesus Christ is born."

He made me a watchman
upon the city wall,
and if I am a Christian,
I am the least of all:
"Go, tell it on the mountain,
"over the hills and everywhere;
"go, tell it on the mountain
"that Jesus Christ is born!"

GOD HAS MADE US THE HANDS OF CHRIST.

ABOUT THE AUTHOR

 Ellen Mongan is a Christian writer and motivational speaker. She hosts the WOW MOM channel on YouTube, Deacon and Dear, and Take 5 podcasts. Ellen writes a monthly column for the *Augusta Chronicle* newspaper, is a blogger for Catholic Mom, and has been a contributor for Women of Grace and Elizabeth Ministry International. She is the founder of WOW MOM and Sisters in Christ. She has spoken on radio and television. Ellen's Bible study, *WOW MOM: A Walk with God*, was published by Covenant Books Inc. and can be found on Amazon and Barnes & Noble.

Ellen is ready to go where God asks her to go and do what He asks her to do because of His amazing grace! She is available for speaking engagements. Her website is www.ellenmongan.com, and her email is wowellen@yahoo.com.

Ellen Mongan has been married forty-seven years to Deacon Patrick Mongan, MD. They have seven adult children, four sons-in-law, two daughters-in-law, fourteen grandchildren. The vocation of wife and mother led her to her ministry, the most important role of all!

CPSIA information can be obtained
at www.ICGtesting.com
Printed in the USA
BVHW020408201022
649778BV00004B/55